D1467016

Citizens' Groups and Broadcasting

Donald L. Guimary

The Praeger Special Studies program—
utilizing the most modern and efficient book
production techniques and a selective
worldwide distribution network—makes
available to the academic, government, and
business communities significant, timely
research in U.S. and international economic, social, and political development.

HE8689.7
.C55G84

Citizens' Groups
and Broadcasting

PRAEGER SPECIAL STUDIES IN U.S. ECONOMIC, SOCIAL, AND POLITICAL ISSUES

Praeger Publishers   New York   Washington   London

Library of Congress Cataloging in Publication Data

Guimary, Donald L
    Citizens' groups and broadcasting

    (Praeger special studies in U. S. economic,
social, and political issues)
    Bibliography: p.
    Includes index
    1. Broadcasting policy—United States—Citizen
participation.   I. Title.
HE8689.7.C55G84   384.54'4'0973   75-8406
ISBN 0-275-01040-6

PRAEGER PUBLISHERS
111 Fourth Avenue, New York, N.Y. 10003, U.S.A.

Published in the United States of America in 1975
by Praeger Publishers, Inc.

All rights reserved

© 1975 by Praeger Publishers, Inc.

Printed in the United States of America

ACKNOWLEDGMENTS

There are a number of persons and organizations who provided assistance and materials for this study. Mrs. A. J. Matkovick, former president of the Greater Cleveland Radio-Television Council; Mrs. Dorothy Lewis, former Coordinator of Listener Activities at the National Association of Broadcasters; May M. Dowell, director of special projects at CBS News; Albert Kramer, of the Citizens' Communications Center; Evelyn Sarson, of Action for Children's Television; Dorothy Palmer, former president of the Minnesota Radio Council; Bill Mears, of KOIN-AM-FM-TV; the National Association of Broadcasters; and members of the Federal Communications Commission. Professors Glen Starlin and Ronald Sherriffs, of the University of Oregon, and Florence Guimary provided considerable encouragement.

Commercial broadcasting has been a public concern since its acceptance as a mass communications medium in the 1920s. In recent years one aspect of this medium—the relationship between the broadcaster and his audience—has come under increased public scrutiny.

The relationship is multifaceted and involves several issues. These issues include how broadcasters should ascertain community interests and needs, how majority and minority audiences can convey their broadcast needs to the broadcaster, and how they can articulate their satisfaction or dissatisfaction with programming.

Another aspect of the problem centers on the Federal Communications Commission. How should the FCC determine if and when a broadcast licensee has served its community adequately, and how can the listening and viewing publics communicate their views to the commission?

A third facet of this relationship involves public participation. Should members of the viewing and listening public participate and attempt to influence programming decisions? Should broadcasters encourage citizen participation such as public input, comments, and suggestions? And if broadcasters seek public comment, how should such information be conveyed and structured?

The traditional relationship between the broadcaster and his publics in some communities—a relationship in which the broadcaster assumes his audience is passive and not demanding—appears to be changing as members of the public become more vocal about programming needs. In certain communities citizens' groups have formed within the last several years to discuss and evaluate the conduct of broadcasting. These groups also have communicated their views to the Federal Communications Commission.

To a certain extent, the traditional interface between the commercial broadcaster and the FCC also appears to be in a state of flux. The FCC is more concerned with the manner and extent to which broadcasters are serving their communities and has, within the last several years, issued more policies and guidelines in that area than in the previous decade. Broadcasters no longer seem to believe the FCC will "rubber stamp" license renewal applications.

Citizens' groups concerned with broadcasting have a history dating back to the 1920s. At one time both the National Association of Broadcasters (NAB) and the FCC supported such groups. The NAB's position has changed; but the FCC, which has not reversed its earlier policy, has tended to vacillate in its degree of inviting the public to participate in broadcast matters.

Because of public participation in commercial broadcasting, the industry has begun to realize that something might be wrong with the system; that perhaps continued reliance on commercial ratings might be incomplete or faulty; that surveying community leaders might not be adequate; that stations should give more thought to how they should ascertain the needs of more segments of their community.

This suggests the importance of citizen involvement in the broadcast industry. Citizens' groups have challenged broadcast licensees legally; participated in renewal proceedings; influenced programming, advertising, and employment policies of stations; and convinced the FCC and the broadcast industry of the effectiveness of public participation, which will probably continue to have an impact on that industry.

But what kind of impact? How can citizens' groups be described, and what is a citizens' group? What do they have in common, and who joins such bodies? Why were they formed; what are their general patters of organization. How did they evolve. What has been the general reaction of broadcasters both public and private, to public participation? What are the long range implications of public involvement in broadcasting. And, if the past is any guideline to the future, what can be expected in future relationships between citizens' groups and broadcasters?

This study surveys citizen involvement in commercial broadcasting to answer those questions. It attempts to determine the historical and current attitudes of broadcast industry leaders, those of the FCC, and how both perceive and react to citizens' groups. After examining the general background of public participation in broadcasting, three case studies of three different citizens' groups are offered.

CONTENTS

Citizens' Groups
and Broadcasting

1

BROADCASTING AND PUBLIC PARTICIPATION

Within the last decade, perhaps with increased awareness of consumers about the use of public resources, citizen participation in the allocation of such resources has increased. Consumerism involves the right of the consumer to be considered in the manufacturing and marketing processes. The environmental movement is usually concerned with the protection and allocation of public resources. Both movements have been directed toward various fields and industries in the United States—including the broadcast industry. Newsweek stated in 1971 that 30 percent of the annual corporate reports by leading corporations in the United States included discussions that year of corporate social responsibility. And the National Association of Manufacturers (NAM), according to the magazine, adopted a "national urban policy," acknowledging that business has an obligation to "participate in the solution" of society's problems.[1] These problems usually involve employment of racial minorities; truth in advertising; less water, air, and noise pollution, and more stringent government regulation.

The broadcast industry, as other industries, has been affected by those two movements: Consumer Reports stated,

The recent wave of license challenges . . . has without question raised the level of program aspiration in most major markets and particularly in those where the jump applications were filed. There is on the whole discernibly more local involvement, more community affairs and educational programming, more news and discussions and more showcasing of minority talent, since the license challenges than there were before.[2]

1

And political scientist Walter Goldstein observed, "After all, if an elite-led revolt of consumers can change the styling of absurdly unsafe automobiles, perhaps an equal revolt can be staged over the uses and misuses of airwaves in the public domain."[3]

Since 1969 the extent of citizen participation in commercial broadcasting has increased significantly. During that year there were two important decisions, one a judicial ruling and the other an informal agreement by a station, which had an impact on the general area of citizens' groups concerned with broadcasting. In the judicial decision involving WLBT-TV, Jackson, Mississippi, the United States Court of Appeals in Washington, D. C., affirmed that citizens' groups do have legal standing to intervene in Federal Communications Commission (FCC) broadcast license renewal cases and encouraged citizens to "take an active interest in the scope and quality of television service. . . ."[4] This became a legal precedent.

In the second case a coalition of citizens' groups was successful in having station KTAL-TV, Texarkana, Texas, change its programing and employment practices. Representatives of racial and religious groups signed a "sweeping private agreement" with the station redressing "racial grievances and guaranteeing future citizen participation in station programming." In return, the coalition dropped its petition to deny the station's license renewal application pending before the FCC and actively supported the station's application.[5]

BROADCASTING UNDER ATTACK

Since those two decisions, citizens' groups have formed to challenge broadcast licensees and have filed petitions with the FCC requesting that the commission refuse renewal of existing licenses or adopt new or different policies regarding broadcasting and public service. In 1971, some 50 petitions to deny license renewals were filed with the FCC, "primarily by community groups in connection with programming for minorities or employment practices."[6] And in June 1972, the commission was "processing more than 100 license challenges—90 percent of which have been filed by predominantly black coalitions."[7] Federal Communications Commissioner R. E. Lee, who served in the agency 19 years, stated, "The regulatory atmosphere is tougher on broadcasting now than it's ever been in my experience."[8] Commissioner Nicholas Johnson observed, "I detect at the FCC a new regard for the consumer that has a chance of taking root." He also noted that the commission has completed the most intensive decade of activity in its history and that "much of the recent decision-making shows every sign of having been distinctly prodded by public representation."[9]

The principal thrust of various citizens' groups appears to center on several issues: more employment of women, blacks, and minorities, the denial of sale and transfer of station ownership, the recognition of legal standing by courts allowing citizens' groups to challenge license renewals legally, increased programming for minority audiences, seeking pledges from station owners to make increased efforts to ascertain minority interests and needs, opening of stations' financial books to license challengers; and the granting of free public service air time to some environmental or antiwar groups.

Nation's Business stated,

Petitions to deny license renewals are being filed with
the FCC on behalf of Negroes, Mexican-Americans,
Puerto Ricans, Indians, Orientals, Gay Liberation,
Women's Lib and various other groups and causes.
Common threads of their complaints concern program-
ming and personnel.[10]

And Broadcasting, the broadcast trade journal, noted that in nearly all cases the protesting groups' complaints

boil down to two or three issues: The broadcaster has
not checked the minority group involved in ascertaining
community needs. . . . The station has not carried
programs that serve the needs of the minority group . . .
The station discriminates against minority groups.

The magazine noted that broadcasters "may never have approached license renewal time with the serenity that critics of the FCC's 'rubber stamp' renewal process thought was warranted."[11]

Probably in response to increased activity by citizens' groups, as well as to assist stations, the FCC issued policies and guidelines to clarify the obligations and responsibilities broadcasters have regarding the relationship between them and their public. Most of these policies centered on how broadcasters should ascertain community interests and needs. For example, more than 10 years ago the FCC issued "The 1960 Programming Policy Statement" in which the broadcaster is obligated to a "good faith" effort to determine the needs of his community.[12] Eleven years later, the FCC issued its 1971 "Primer on Ascertainment of Community Problems by Broadcast Applicants." The primer discussed how stations can ascertain community needs and issues.[13] And in 1972 the commission issued a pamphlet, "The Public and Broadcasting," which described in detail how citizens could become involved in license renewal proceedings. This manual appeared to be designed mainly for the public rather than for broadcasters.[14]

William Ray, chief of the FCC's Complaints and Compliance Division, observed that since 1960 the number of broadcast licenses revoked by the commission has increased significantly compared with a low number from the period 1934-60, estimating that about 90 licenses were revoked or not renewed since 1960 for a variety of reasons. In other words, the increase in license revocations appeared to parallel the increased interest in consumerism.[15]

Placed in a different perspective, some citizens' groups argued that perhaps broadcasting was too important to be left to broadcasters. Albert H. Kramer, director of the Citizens Communications Center, a private legal resource organization in Washington, D.C., said in 1971,

> "The beneficial aspect (of the citizens movement) is that people are involved in the process of government, in the things that affect their lives. You begin to get a functioning adversary system." He added that citizens groups are not in the decision-making process, but they are making inroads on the power to influence decisions—that that's the name of the game.[16]

One year later, in 1972, Kramer said, "once a lot of people learn about their rights, it's hard to keep them from exercising them. People want back more control over their lives."[17]

Perhaps to exercise this control, some citizens' groups, according to Broadcasting, "have discovered a point of entry to broadcast regulation and they are exploiting it with increasing sophistication and skill." The journal referred to citizens participating in license renewal proceedings by filing a petition to deny renewal.[18] One thoughtful broadcaster observed,

> Nobody wants to change. But change is coming, maybe faster than we want it. Yes, broadcasting is changing. We must recognize that change is coming and be ready to bend.[19]

On December 18, 1972, Clay T. Whitehead, director of the Office of Telecommunications Policy and executive assistant to President Richard Nixon, proposed federal legislation that would amend the 1934 Communications Act. Whitehead's speech suggested that Congress pass

> a bill to amend the Communications Act of 1934 to
> provide that licenses for the operation of a broad-
> cast station shall be issued for a term of five years,
> and to establish orderly procedures for the considera-
> tion of applications for the renewal of such licenses. [20]

The bill, which was sent to the Office of Management and Budget for
clearance to Congress, would have provided protection against challengers (and these would include citizens' groups) at license renewal
time. It proposed that the FCC would be required to determine that
a licensee's record did not warrant renewal before it could call the
renewal proceedings and would prohibit the commission from setting
quantitative standards for judging renewal applications. [21] Broadcasting
said the Nixon administration's license renewal proposal "answers
a prayer broadcasters have directed toward Washington for years. "[22]

Indicating the seriousness with which he viewed the current tur-
moil in broadcasting, Whitehead stated in his December 1972 speech:

> I am particularly concerned about testimony (in Con-
> gress) on broadcast license renewal legislation. Broad-
> casters are making a determined push for some reason-
> able measure of license renewal security. Right now
> they are living over a trap door the FCC can spring at
> the drop of a competing application or other renewal
> challenge. That is a tough position to be in, and, con-
> sidering all the fuss about so-called "intimidation, "
> you would think that there wouldn't be much opposition
> to giving broadcasters a little more insulation from
> government's hand on that trap door. But there is op-
> position. Some tough questions will be asked—even by
> those who are sympathetic to broadcasters. Questions
> about minority groups' needs and interests. Questions
> about violence. Questions about children's programming;
> about reruns; about commercials; about objectivity in
> news and public affairs programming—in short, all
> questions about broadcasters' performance in fulfilling
> their public trust. These are questions the public is
> asking. [23]

It is against this background of public participation in broadcasting and the broadcasters' concern about citizen involvement that
this study is directed.

A basic assumption of this investigation is that public participation in broadcasting has provided a valid link between the broadcaster
and his various publics. Such participation is a real concern to

broadcasters, who have organized themselves on an industrywide
collective basis for protection against petitions filed by citizens'
groups. As a result, broadcasters are seeking relief and protection
in a political context by asking Congress to change the 1934 Communications Act to extend the license renewal period from three to
five years.

A related assumption of broader scope is that the attitudes of
broadcasters toward citizen participation are part of a larger question:
how do broadcasters view themselves and the role of their station in
the community and in society. Before these assumptions can be further
developed, the information offered in this study needs to be placed in
perspective and set within a general framework and context. An overview including definitions of the public interest, attitudes of broadcasters, economics of broadcasting, and the FCC therefore will be
offered.

ARE THE PUBLICS SATISFIED?

Has the public or have the various publics been satisfied with
the commercial programming practices in this country? There are
several ways to address this broad question: from the point of view
of the broadcaster, from the point of view of the FCC, from a theo-
retical viewpoint that implies a broad definition of "the public interest,"
and from the point of view of minority publics or groups that have
articulated their opinions. No viewpoint is wholly satisfactory since
there seems to be no absolute answer to that question. And the answers
offered by those concerned may be from a self-serving or conditioned
perspective. Yet to answer "Who speaks for the public?", a tentative
extrapolation needs to be offered, at least for this study.

The broadcaster tends to respond with results of commercial
rating services. These ratings are determined by sampling the specific
viewing or listening habits of various segments of the U.S. population.
The ratings are designed to project statistically the size of target
audiences consuming specific programs. They are not designed to
ask audiences what they would like to hear or view. And if large
enough audience segments consume specified programs, advertisers
will be attracted to the programs and purchase commercial time.
Consequently the broadcaster is led to believe that his audience is
satisfied—or at least satisfied to the extent that it is viewing or listening to the programs offered and to the extent that such programs are
supported by advertisers. The general response of the broadcasters
has been that they have been giving the public what it wants. This
will be discussed further in the section on the attitudes of broadcasters.

WHO SPEAKS FOR THE PUBLIC?

To answer the question "Are the publics satisfied" implies that
the publics can speak for themselves and that their voices can be
heard by the broadcasters. Various publics have articulated their
opinions regarding commercial broadcasting. But no one speaks for
the public. Some vocal groups, perhaps for selfish interests, have
expressed their dissatisfaction, although these groups rarely claim
to speak for the general public. The program ratings used by broadcasters tend to offer limited value in that only viewing habits are
determined and projected. The FCC, as a government agency with
the responsibility to represent the public interest, tends to issue
policies and decisions only in specific instances when a commission
regulation is violated or when the commission is influenced by special
interest groups, including broadcasters.

In September 1971, Life reported the results of a special Louis
Harris poll commissioned by the magazine to determine public attitudes
toward television. The results of that poll, which can be said to
represent the views of that particular public, indicated that viewers
felt that entertainment shows, which account for more than two-thirds
of all television programs, generally were "discouraging."[24]

Another citizens' group, the National Citizens Committee for
Broadcasting, conducted a three-month survey covering 16 nations
regarding the extent of network programs for children on weekdays.
In an article on the survey, the New York Times reported that the
United States is the only major nation that does not provide network
programs for children on weekday afternoons. It also reported that
"American commercial network programs for children are marked
by a high degree of over commercialization and a low level of informational content compared with other countries."[25]

Other citizens' groups have voiced their opinions, which generally
tend to be critical, of broadcast practices. Such groups include the
American Council for Better Broadcasts, the National Association
for Better Broadcasting, the Foundation to Improve Television, Action
for Children's Television, the United Church of Christ Communication
Section, and the Citizens Communication Center. These will be described in Chapter 5.

There also have been more militant groups voicing demands.
These groups include the Columbus Broadcasting Coalition in Ohio,
the Coalition for the Enforcement of Equality in Television and Radio
in New Mexico, and the Chinese Media Committee in San Francisco.
The existence of such groups and their increasing number could suggest
that more citizens have formed to concern themselves with commercial
broadcast practices.

In summary, one conclusion that can be offered is that no one speaks for the general public; various publics can only speak for themselves—if they so desire. There are many diverse majority and minority publics. The groups cited above have been formed expressly to concern themselves with broadcasting, and their numbers appear to have increased. Although they represent a particular point of view— a need for improvement in broadcast practices—no one can claim to speak for the general public.

THE PUBLIC INTEREST

> The public interest may be what men would choose if they saw clearly, thought rationally, acted disinterested and benevolently.
>
> Walter Lippmann

The second point of view in providing a general overview and framework to discuss citizen participation involves a broad definition of "the public interest." The FCC has refused to offer specifically or formally a definition and prefers to apply that phrase only in selected cases. This is in keeping with the District Court of Appeals in Washington, D. C., which stated in 1946,

> It would be difficult, if not impossible to formulate a precise and comprehensive definition of the term "public interest, convenience or necessity," and it has been said often and properly by the courts that the facts of each (FCC) case must be examined and must govern its determination.[26]

Although the FCC and the courts have refused to define that concept, several broad definitions entailing "the public interest" have been offered by other sources. Gilbert Seldes, the late broadcasting academician and student of the mass media, offered an insightful concept:

> The public interest is to give life, which includes the power of adaptation and growth, to the essential values of the past so that they can form the character of the future. . . . Whatever engages more of the interest of the individual, whatever tends to enlarge his understanding of life, whatever makes him able to use more of his

faculties and to "live more abundantly" is good; and whatever limits, restricts and diminishes is bad.[27]

Seldes was referring specifically to the broadcast medium when he offered that definition.

Related to the definition offered by Seldes was a statement of the public interest offered by the Pilkington Commission, which studied the British Broadcasting Corporation and its audiences in England in 1962:

> No one can say he is giving the public what it wants, unless the public knows the whole range of possibilities which television can offer, and from this range, chooses what it wants to see. For a choice is only free if the field of choice is not unnecessarily restricted. The subject matter of television is to be found in the whole scope and variety of human awareness and experience. If viewers— the public—are thought as "the mass audience," or "the majority" they will be offered only the average of common experience and awareness; the "ordinary"; the common-place—for what all know and do is, by definition, common-place. They will be kept unaware of what lies beyond the average of experience; their field of choice will be limited. In time they may come to like only what they know. But it will always be true, that had they been offered a wider range from which to choose, they might and often would have chosen otherwise, and with greater enjoyment. . . .

> "To give the public what it wants" is a misleading phrase; misleading because as commonly used it has the appearance of an appeal to democratic principle, but the appearance is deceptive. It is in fact patronizing and arrogant, in that it claims to know what the public is, but defines it as no more than the mass audience; and in that it claims to know what it wants, but limits its choice to the average of experience. In this sense we reject it utterly. If there is a sense in which it should be used, it is this: what the public wants and what it has the right to get is the freedom from the widest possible range of programme matter. Anything less than that is deprivation. . . . [28]

Although the Pilkington Commission's statement was directed toward the British broadcasting system and its public, its definition would seem to apply to the U.S. system and its audiences.

The applicability of that statement and the manner in which U.S. commercial broadcasters have served their audiences "by giving the public what it wants" has been reinforced by Ralph Stavins who wrote,

> Having raised the viewing public on a visual diet of
> verbal twaddle and violent rabble, TV has undoubtedly
> conditioned our expectations for whatever will be shown.
> Once we are trained to see certain things, we not only
> expect to continue to see them, but we begin to wish to
> see them repeated. That is, in a majority of cases, we
> demand from the future what we have been given in the
> past. Psychologically, this is called repetition compulsion.
> Physically, it is referred to as conditioned response.
> These laws—operative in the majority of cases—constitute
> formal behavioral principles. [29]

If the definitions offered by Seldes and the Pilkington Commission, as well as the pessimistic view of Stavins, are applied to the general broadcast practices—which are designed to reach the largest possible audiences for mainly entertainment purposes—it would appear that those practices have not been serving the public interest.

In summary, the phrase "public interest" cannot be precisely defined, as the courts have noted. Yet broad, general definitions have been offered. As Les Brown succinctly observed, "The public interest may be hard to define but it is not without meaning." [30]

ECONOMIC CONSIDERATION

Before discussing the attitudes of broadcasters and the FCC in this brief overview of the relationship between broadcasters and the public, one further aspect should be presented: the economics of the broadcast industry.

Because the U.S. broadcast system operates on a competitive, free enterprise basis after an FCC license has been granted, commercial broadcasters first consider economics. The tendency to design programming for the largest possible mass audiences for the advertisers is strong. This means that minority publics, regardless of their size, tend to be neglected. Reaching for the largest possible audience means providing programs that minimize controversial topics, or those that might offend the largest viewing public. Fred Friendly, former president of Columbia Broadcasting System (CBS)

News, has observed that it is more profitable to televise an "intellectual ghetto" of nighttime entertainment rather than sometimes controversial documentaries and news specials, which sponsors are less willing to support. [31]

Another result of the economic consideration is the tendency of many local stations to use network programs instead of producing local programs dealing with community topics. Describing the relationship between the local broadcasters and the national networks, Whitehead said, " . . . all that many affiliates do is flip the switch in the control room to 'network,' throw the 'switch' in the mailroom to forward viewer complaints to the network, sit back, and enjoy the fruits of a very profitable business."[32] Whitehead stressed that local stations should be held accountable for all programming, including that of networks.

It is more convenient and profitable for local stations to use network programs. By relying on network programming, local stations do not need to employ large full-time production crews on union salaries and do not need to do as much local scheduling. Moreover, local stations are compensated by the networks and the advertisers for airing national advertisements. As Sydney Head aptly stated, economic factors "conspire against local programming."[33]

ATTITUDES OF BROADCASTERS

It is difficult to determine and evaluate the attitudes of broadcasters regarding citizen involvement in programming, employment, and other station matters. There are simply too many broadcasters; and the attitudes with which they view public participation are determined by a variety of factors: their personal predispositions, their attitudes toward the FCC and government regulation, the profitability of their stations, how they define "the public interest," and the history of their stations and their relationships with the community.

Nevertheless, to provide a general framework and perspective this study does attempt to determine general reactions and patterns of some broadcasters, network executives, and the National Association of Broadcasters (NAB) regarding public participation. These will be compared with how broadcasters reacted toward citizen involvement in the 1930s and 1940s. For example, some individual broadcasters acknowledged the value of working with citizens' groups and noted that they are now aware of community concerns of which they previously had not been cognizant. This contemporary view is in consonance with the views of many broadcasters in the 1930s and 1940s who encouraged citizen involvement in listening councils. This early encouragement probably was prompted by several factors: broadcasters were anxious to promote the medium; they were receptive to public feedback and suggestions; and they encouraged educators, schools, and other community organizations to use broadcast programs for civic purposes.

To place the attitudes of broadcasters regarding citizen involvement into some framework and determine if those attitudes fall into predictive patterns along a "like/dislike public participation continuum," a crude hypothesis is offered: the manner in which the broadcaster views citizen involvement is part of a larger question involving how he perceives his role in the community. If the station manager or network executive views his organization as an active, viable institution in the community and is seeking to help improve society, he probably would be receptive to community and citizen suggestions, comments, and feedback. In other words, such a broadcast official realizes he could learn from his publics and would be willing to work with local groups.

On the other hand, if a broadcaster is more concerned with profits (providing minimal local programming), he may perceive his station as "doing an adequate job" and would not be receptive to comments and suggestions from the community. Such a station manager may feel he needs no assistance and would resent unsolicited opinions, feeling they were intrusive. This station manager probably would exert a minimal effort to ascertain community interests and to comply with the FCC's 1971 "Primer on Ascertainment of Community Problems by Broadcast Applicants,"[34] which describes in detail how broadcasters may or may not determine local issues to use as a guideline in local programming.

In general, most network executives and spokesmen for the NAB regard public participation with a certain reservation, if not hostility. In correspondence with this investigator, in speeches, and in trade journals, broadcast leaders have spoken out against the principle of encouraging citizens' groups.

Yet on an individual basis, some network and station officials have entered into working agreements with members of citizens' groups. The general pattern of contemporary broadcasters is in contrast with the manner in which the NAB viewed citizen participation in the 1930s and 1940s. At that time, the NAB encouraged public participation and employed a full-time person to establish radio listening councils in major cities in the nation.

It should be noted, however, that some station managers who apparently view their facilities as active in the community, do make a positive effort to ascertain community interests and needs. Thomas Baldwin and Stuart Surlin in "A Study of Broadcast Station License Application Exhibits on Ascertainment of Community Needs" examined

eight methods by which broadcasters determine community interests.
They are by participating in the community, contacting community
leaders, employing advisory councils, using mail surveys, using
phone surveys, holding personal interviews, inviting letters, and
having employees engage in local speaking engagements.[35] The authors
reported that of all radio and television stations in their sample of
227, 9 percent used advisory councils to help determine local programming guidelines. In the top 30 television markets, the percentage
using councils rose to 19. But when considering only the AM radio
stations using councils, the figure dropped to 3 percent.

In an attempt to apply their findings to Oregon stations, a
questionnaire was mailed to 87 radio and 12 television stations in
1971 to determine how stations determined community interests. The
questionnaire asked six questions: (1) does the station have a council;
(2) its size; (3) how the council meets; (4) when it was formed; (5)
is the panel considered beneficial; (6) if a panel is not used, how are
community interests determined.

A total of 46 completed forms were returned from 39 radio and
eight television stations, a response of 50 percent. Six of the eight
television stations reported using citizens' advisory councils; only
three of the 39 radio stations said they used panels. The size of the
councils for the television stations range from 12 to 25 members.
Most meet monthly or quarterly. Two were formed in 1968, one in
1969, and two were organized before 1965. A majority of the stations
not using advisory panels said they used surveys, interviews with
community leaders, and community participation to determine community needs and interests.[36]

The suggestions, comments, and feedback that these advisory
councils provide are considered by station managers in determining
local programming. There is no assurance, however, that the information and suggestions provided actually will be implemented;
and it could be argued that stations use such councils for public
relations purposes.

There is one more aspect regarding the views of broadcasters
on public involvement that should be discussed in this overview of the
relationship between the broadcaster and his audiences. This view is
from the perspective of viewing the broadcaster as a businessman.

Raymond Bauer noted that an economic man's view of his actions
are determined by rational economic goals. "Businessmen do indeed
follow their own self-interest. They do it consciously and continu-
ously."[37] Yet broadcasters, to a degree greater than their counter-
parts in other industries, are charged with a public responsibility
to serve their communities since they use a public resource. John
Pfiffner and Robert Presthus noted that business groups traditionally
have had more influence with government agencies than the public.[38]

This view is reinforced by Seymour Lipset, who noted, "In every country, businessmen have well developed organizations and a large part of the press represents their viewpoint."[39]

It would be appropriate at this time to consider briefly the role of the FCC, since the attitudes of broadcasters are in part determined by their perception of the commission and by the degree of FCC regulation.

THE FEDERAL COMMUNICATIONS COMMISSION

In terms of regulation, the FCC, as other federal regulatory agencies, has three main functions: to inform the industry and other regulated groups of the objectives of public policy on regulation, to discover and issue rules and regulations affecting this policy, and to enforce the rules by adjudicating controversies between the public and the interest regulated or by prosecuting policy violaters.[40]

The commission operates on funds granted by Congress. And congressmen, from time to time, have been known to exert pressure on the FCC whenever the agency is perceived as acting in ways that threaten broadcasters. Some congressmen own interests in broadcast properties; and, since during elections legislators naturally seek broadcast exposure, it has been argued that some members of Congress have sympathized more with the broadcast industry than with the FCC.[41] Pfiffner and Presthus noted,

> . . . there is a tendency of independent regulatory
> agencies to surrender their regulatory zeal as they
> age, and to become more and more the protagonists
> of a clientele industry, and less and less the vigilant
> defenders of the welfare of the consumers or the gen-
> eral public. All too often, those who are supposedly
> being regulated actually regulate their nominal reg-
> ulators.[42]

Regarding public participation and public satisfaction with broadcast practices, the FCC tends to take a neutral stance unless specific and valid complaints and petitions have been filed against a particular station. As a quasi-judicial regulatory agency, the commission cannot assume absolute positions except in rule-making decisions, and it cannot assume the role of a program censor.

Individual commission members, however, when speaking for themselves, have taken positions; and these views tend to vary with the individual philosophic definition of how a public resource should be governed, the role of government agency as a guardian of that resource, and the role of government in relation to business.

The FCC has been accused of failing to exercise consistently its regulatory authority. Critics of the commission accuse the FCC of issuing decisions more favorable to the broadcast industry than to the consuming public.[43] Such criticism includes the charges that the commission traditionally has renewed "automatically" broadcast licenses without critically reviewing the licensees' records;[44] that the FCC has not enforced its own regulations and policies;[45] and that the commission has not consulted the listening or viewing public regarding how broadcasters have or have not served community interests.[46]

The FCC occasionally has issued guidelines and policies for broadcasters on how they could serve their communities. For example, in 1960 the commission issued "The 1960 Programming Policy Statement," which offered guidelines stating, "The broadcaster is obligated to make a positive, diligent and continuing effort, in good faith, to determine the tastes, needs and desires of the public in his community and to provide programming to meet those needs and interests."[47] This was held to be a personal duty of the broadcaster "and may not be avoided by delegation of the responsibility to others."[48] Another example is the FCC's 1971 Primer, mentioned earlier, and the commission's "The Public and Broadcasting," a short pamphlet describing the responsibilities of the licensee, the commission, and the public. The manual apparently was issued to help the public and discuss in detail how one could participate in license renewal proceedings. Both the commission and its publications and policies will be discussed in detail in Chapter 4.

The commission has had its detractors, and it has had shortcomings. But on the plus side, it has issued policies that tend to benefit the various publics. As noted earlier, because of the increased tempo of the consumer movement, the FCC may alter its traditional tendency of favoring the industry. FCC Commissioner Johnson, in predicting future changes in the commission, cited as examples the FCC's ban on cigarette advertising, its decision to study children's television programming, and its agreements giving citizens' committees a voice in programming.[49]

SUMMARY

Realizing that these brief perspectives are not comprehensive and that they represent only the general viewpoints of three segments involved with broadcasting, four tentative conclusions can be offered.

First, it would appear that a pattern has developed concerning the lack of public participation in broadcasting. And because of this pattern, citizens have formed various committees and organizations designed to influence stations and the FCC. These citizens' groups range from well-established organizations formed to achieve long range goals to interim, transient groups organized to obtain immediate, short term objectives.

Second, broadcasters as a group tend to place more reliance on ratings; and, because of their concern for economics, they have developed the pattern of not encouraging public participation; though through the encouragement of the NAB, broadcasters once supported citizen involvement. Some broadcasters, on an individual basis, have agreed to work with citizens' groups to obtain their views on programming and on the role of the station in the community.

Third, the FCC has a pattern of inconsistency regarding citizen participation, and only within the last several years has the commission resumed support of public involvement.

Finally, it should be noted that public reaction and general satisfaction with commercial programming practices has been diverse and varied. It would be incorrect to conclude that all members of radio and television audiences are satisfied, and it would be equally incorrect to state that all are dissatisfied. Both broadcasters and articulate citizens' groups can and have cited statistics to support their arguments.

NOTES

1. "The American Corporation Under Fire," Newsweek, May 24, 1971, pp. 74-85.

2. "Making FCC's Mission Impossible," Consumer Reports 35, No. 2 (February 1970): 110.

3. Walter Goldstein, "Network Television and Political Change: Two Issues In Democratic Theory," Western Political Quarterly 20 (December 1967), p. 885.

4. Robert Lewis Shayon, "Chickens and Foxes," Saturday Review, October 16, 1971, p. 73.

5. "The Texarkana Agreement as a Model Strategy for Citizen Participation in FCC License Renewals," Harvard Journal on Legislation 7, No. 4 (May 1970): 627.

6. U.S. Federal Communications Commission, The FCC in Fiscal 1971, Annual Report, p. 8.

7. "Blacks vs. Broadcasters," Newsweek, June 19, 1972, p. 84.

8. "Inside the FCC," Television/Radio Age, February 22, 1971, p. 77.

9. "Johnson Praises FCC Concern for Consumer," Broadcasting, February 1, 1971, p. 44.

10. "Death of an Industry?" Nation's Business 60, No. 5 (May 1972): 28.

11. "Signs of Changing Times in Renewals," Broadcasting, May 17, 1971, p. 34.

12. U.S. Federal Communications Commission, Network Programming Inquiry, Report and Statement of Policy, July 29, 1960.

13. U.S. Federal Communications Commission, FCC Reports, Docket 18774, February 18, 1971.

14. U.S. Federal Communications Commission, The Public and Broadcasting, Procedural Manual in Federal Register, Part III 37, No. 190 (September 29, 1972): 20510-18.

15. William Ray, private interview held during meeting of Oregon Association of Broadcasters, Portland, Oregon, November 5, 1971.

16. Broadcasting, May 17, 1971, op. cit., p. 35.

17. "Any Ceiling Now in Sight on the Price of Settling Price Protests?" Broadcasting, May 29, 1972, p. 18.

18. Ibid.

19. "The Struggle Over Broadcast Access (II)," Broadcasting, September 27, 1971, p. 24.

20. "The Dust Hasn't Settled After Speech," Broadcasting, January 1, 1973, p. 18.

21. Ibid.

22. Ibid, p. 24.

23. Clay Whitehead, speech delivered to the Sigma Delta Chi Luncheon, Indianapolis, Indiana, December 18, 1972.

24. "The Heaviest Viewers are the Lonely and Alienated," Life, September 10, 1971, pp. 42-3.

25. New York Times article printed in the Eugene (Oregon) Register-Guard, July 5, 1971.

26. Sydney Head, Broadcasting in America, A Survey of Television and Radio (Boston: Houghton Mifflin, 1972), p. 366.

27. Gilbert Seldes, The New Mass Media (Washington, D.C.: Public Affairs Press, 1968), pp. 62-7.

28. Ronald H. Coase, "The Economics of Broadcasting and Public Policy," in The Crisis of the Regulatory Commissions, Paul W. MacAvoy, ed. (New York: W. W. Norton & Co., 1970), p. 97.

29. Ralph L. Stavins, ed., Television Today: The End of Communication and The Death of Community (Washington, D.C.: Institute for Policy Studies, 1969), p. 74.

30. Les Brown, Television, The Business Behind the Box (New York: Harcourt, Brace Jovanovich, Inc., 1971), p. 211.

31. The Oregonian, October 13, 1971.

32. Whitehead, op. cit.

33. Head, op. cit.

34. FCC Reports, op. cit.

35. Thomas F. Baldwin and Stuart Surlin, "A Study of Broadcast Station License Application Exhibits on Ascertainment of Community Needs," Journal of Broadcasting 14, No. 4 (spring 1970): 164.

36. Don Guimary, "Oregon TV, Radio Stations Weigh Public Tastes," The Oregon Broadcaster, 17, No. 7 (January 1972): 3.

37. Raymond Bauer, Itheil de Sola Pool, and L. A. Dexter, American Business and Public Policies (New York: Atherton Press, 1963), p. 472.

38. John Pfiffner and Robert Presthus, Public Administration (New York: The Ronald Press, 1967), p. 443.

39. Seymour Lipset, Political Man (New York: Doubleday, 1960), p. 194.

40. Pfiffner and Presthus, op. cit.

41. Drew Pearson, The Case Against Congress (New York: Pocket Books, 1969), p. 178.

42. Ibid.

43. "Making FCC's Mission Impossible," Consumer Reports, op. cit.

44. Nicholas Johnson, How To Talk Back To Your Television Set (New York: Bantam Books, 1970), p. 164.

45. Charles Stepmann, Radio, Television and Society (New York: Oxford University Press, 1950), p. 37.

46. Harry Skornia, Television and Society (New York: McGraw-Hill Co., 1965), p. 80.

47. FCC 1960 Network Programming Statement of Policy, op. cit.

48. Ibid.

49. Broadcasting, February 1, 1971, op. cit.

2

Public criticism of commercial broadcasting is not a new phenomenon in this country. Ralph Lewis Smith has traced the formation of broadcast criticism back to the 1920s.[1] And in the 1930s a group of men and women representing various organizations formed the Radio Council on Children's Programs. The council raised such questions as: What is the actual number of children's programs? What stations carry what programs that are sponsored and merchandized? What effects are locally produced programs having on the children and parents in their respective communities? Are there enough good programs to satisfy the natural demands of active-minded children?[2]

Questions similar to those have been raised 40 years later by Action for Children's Television and the National Committee on Better Broadcasting. These two recent groups will be discussed in Chapter 5. This chapter will discuss the historical development of the citizens' movement.

In his study of professional criticism of broadcasting, Smith described the citizen councils as an "interesting development in lay criticism coming out of the late thirties and early forties. The original motivation for their fomulation was a growing concern over the effect of radio on young people. . . . Although listener councils have never been a major force, they represent a unique attempt to encourage lay criticism, and could, conceivably, become the source of a strong, intelligent, public voice which would improve American broadcasting." He suggested that the listener council concept needed to be examined.[3]

FRAMEWORK OF CITIZENS' GROUPS

Before discussing citizens' broadcast councils as broadcast-related phenomena, it would first be helpful to examine citizens' groups from a sociological perspective to provide a general framework of the range of participatory associations.

In describing citizen participation in voluntary associations, Arthur Jacoby and Nicholas Babchuck noted, "Sociologists frequently classify voluntary organizations as being 'instrumental' or 'expressive' according to their goals. Instrumental organizations pursue activities primarily as a means of achieving some goal, such as preservation of natural resources. Expressive organizations pursue activities for their own sake, such as specific types of recreation."[4] Membership in such groups probably would be drawn from the upper middle class, as in the case of environmental movement groups, which tend to have well-educated memberships.[5]

Regarding associations, Gabriel Almond and Sidney Verba observed,

> Voluntary associations are the prime means by which the function of mediating between the individual and the state is performed. Through them the individual is able to relate himself effectively and meaningfully to the political systems. These associations help him avoid the dilemma of being either a parochial, cut off from political influence, or an isolated and powerless individual, manipulated and mobilized by the mass institutions of politics and government.[6]

The two authors also noted that if the citizen is a member of a voluntary instrumental association, "he is involved in the broader social world but is less dependent upon and less controlled by his political system. This is so for several reasons. The association of which he is a member can represent his needs and demands before the government. It can make the government more chary of engaging in activities that would harm the individual."[7]

The general function or purpose of citizens' councils or advisory committees as instrumental associations can be addressed from at least two points of view: from that of a citizen as a consumer and from a political perspective involving power and visibility. For the former, Elliot Krause stated, "The consumer as participant can guarantee that services will be adequate, appropriate and utilized."[8]

For the latter view, which tends to support the observation offered by Almond and Verba, the Center for the Study of Democratic Institutions wrote,

The work of government as manager of the public resources of the nation becomes one of its major tasks.
Decisions about their common property—water, power,
air space, channels of communication, atomic energy,
forests—affect each man's well being. But the people
have lost control over these decisions to the professional
management or bureaucracies . . .the great danger is
that an entrenched professional bureaucracy will become
shortsighted in its perception of the good. . . . Professional planners and managers cannot be dispensed with.
But some means of public participation, however inadequate,
would at least offer the beginning of a system of planning
that would encompass a broader vision and a deeper relation of democratic ideals.[9]

Similarly, sociologist Herbert Gans suggested,

The American political-bureaucratic complex must be
restructured so that it will attend to the demands of
average citizens rather than those of the best organized
to apply maximal political pressure or the largest campaign contributions. The right combination of central-
ization and citizen control has to be found to make this
complex both effective and democratic, responsive to
majority rule as well as to the rights of minorities,
at state and inferior levels as well as the federal levels.[10]

Citizens' groups should also be evaluated for their efficacy;
some are more effective than others. The results of such organizations
can be only as effective as their members and their group efforts.
Roberta Sigal, who worked with a citizens' committee for planning
schools, characterized the committee as slow, accepting of administrative goals, depending on experts, failing to generate its own
ideas, and avoiding conflicts within the committee.[11]
    Along the same lines, Krause found that poor people participating
in citizens' boards of communication action programs achieved little.
He quotes Frank Riessman,

When the poor have become extensively involved in
active planning or in community action work, the
administrators have found that things got very complicated, routine decisions were questioned, conflict
escalated, and timetables were delayed which in some
cases cost money for the urban renewal agency.[12]

He noted that local and federal officials could circumvent, frustrate, and even thwart the goals of such committees.

Since citizens' broadcast councils are concerned with a government agency, the FCC, and with the manner in which broadcasters use a public resource, the airwaves, it would seem proper to regard the councils as serving two functions: to aid the viewing and listening publics as consumers and to improve, expedite, and assist the political process and the government.

There are at least several types of citizens' groups involved with broadcasting. One is community groups established to achieve long range goals involving local stations and seeking to work with broadcasters on a friendly basis. This type of group, from a sociological perspective, uses a combination of both expressive and instrumental elements.

The second general category of groups contains instrumental associations that have been formed to achieve specific goals. In this category are groups formed on a nationwide basis to influence both local and national broadcasters, as well as the FCC and other government agencies; resource groups providing legal and support services and expertise to various community organizations on a nonprofit basis; and groups having a transitory nature formed to achieve short range objectives (and which are not concerned with the type of relationships they have with broadcasters). Some groups represent the interests of racial minorities, but others are not concerned with such interests.

THE COUNCIL CONCEPT

Before discussing the development of councils, however, it would be best to first define the main functions of the council concept since such organizations can be interpreted variously. Charles Siepmann explained a council's functions in the following:

> To collect and publicize essential facts on the present state of broadcasting; to facilitate and encourage discriminating listening to worthwhile programs; to bring pressure on stations to eliminate abuses; to voice the needs of the community by preparing blueprints of worthwhile programs to be executed by a station; to provide listeners with opportunity to meet and to discuss their interests in radio; by means of bulletins and circulars to alert listeners to important developments in radio; to carry its members' views to the Federal Communications Commission, whether with reference to the matters

of policy raised in public hearings before the FCC, or
to the renewal of a given station's license; to influence
not only radio but the press by correspondence and
prepared articles as a social force. [13]

A list complementing the above was offered by Judith Waller,
director of public affairs and education with the National Broadcasting
Company (NBC) in 1950. Her nine-point list was adopted by the Radio
Council of Greater Cleveland in Ohio, which "fairly well represents
the aims of all councils." Following are four points not mentioned
in Siepmann's definition:

To coordinate the interests of civic, religious and
educational and business organizations to encourage
the presentation of more radio programs which meet
with the high standards of entertainment, artistry, and
morality for adults and children;

To create and maintain patronage for sponsors of radio
programs who broadcast programs meeting the standards
recommended by this (NBC) organization;

To stimulate and aid parents in assuming responsibility
for children's radio and entertainment;

Through open discussion to develop recommendations to
radio stations of standards deemed to be desirable for
broadcasting and in the public interest, convenience and
necessity. [14]

These two definitions seem to encompass the main functions
of citizens' councils, especially if the term "television" also were
inserted. What Siepmann and Waller advocated more than 20 years
ago could be applied to current broadcasting stations and their
communities.

COUNCIL ORIGINS

Historically, no one precisely knows when or how the phrase
"radio council" was first used, although the first formal appearance
of the term was recorded as early as 1922. That year the University
of Chicago, Northwestern University, and DePaul University, together
with NBC, CBS, Mutual Network, the Rockefeller Foundation, and

the Carnegie Corporation agree to form and finance the University Broadcasting Council for four years. Radio stations WLS, WJJD, and WIND also participated in the pioneer venture in educational broadcasting. Its goals were "to create, develop, schedule radio programs of an educational or cultural nature and to conduct experiments and research in education in radio."[15]

It was probably the group listening approach—which emanated from educational broadcasting—that helped create the early radio councils and the mood from which the citizens' groups originated.

The group listening approach also was affiliated and later supported by the Educational Radio Project and the Federal Forum Project of the U.S. Office of Education. The Federal Works Projects Administration (WPA) worked with the National Youth Administration and the University of Wisconsin in a "Radio Study Groups Projects" in 1936-37, which continued until World War II.

These early educational broadcast listening groups have been discussed by Frank Hill and John Ohliger. Hill estimated at the time there were "at least 15,000 organized groups meeting together to hear radio programs, and their activities touch from 300,000 to 500,000 Americans."[16] He also observed, "Listening groups developed at a slower pace in the United States than in Great Britain primarily because the American system of broadcasting is decentralized and contains no provision for nationwide distribution of all programs."[17]

As a probable result of the concern of early education broadcasting, citizens' groups began in the mid-1930s when there was a "good deal of agitation by various organizations concerning children's programming." This agitation resulted in the New York organization of a group representing organizations and educators—the Radio Council on Children's Programs cited earlier.[18]

NAB-SUPPORTED COUNCILS

The Radio Council on Children's Programs subsequently made a national survey to answer some persistent questions under a $1,500 NAB grant. Dorothy Lewis, vice chairman of the Radio Council and national chairman of the National Society of New England Women conducted the study. After she completed her report, Lewis in 1944 joined the NAB staff as coordinator of listener activities. She has been credited with having been "probably responsible for or has aided in the formation of 25 to 30 active radio councils in such places as Nashville, The Twin Cities of Minneapolis and St. Paul, Des Moines, Cedar Rapids, Omaha, Cleveland, Kansas City, St. Louis, Portland, Seattle, Salt Lake City, Wichita, Reno, and Utica, to name only a few."[19]

In 1942 Lewis noted that the groundwork for radio councils "has been laid for such councils in about 120 cities in the United States as well as Canada." They were composed of "civic, autonomous bodies made up of elected representatives, men and women, from club, civic, and educational groups of the community, sometimes numbering 100,000 potential members. On every council board are representatives of the radio industry to preserve a working democracy. Dues are nominal, contributed by member groups. . . . Broadly speaking, the councils' purposes are to interpret the problems of radio broadcasting to the listeners and to bring to the radio industry the wishes of the public."[20]

Two years later she estimated there were 50 such councils. "Most radio councils allowed individual members as well. The average number of potential members runs from 100,000 to 150,000 per council. Altogether, some 2,500,000 persons are affiliated in this manner with radio, actively supporting and promoting the industry. Thus, listeners and broadcasters are working together 'to the public interest, convenience and necessity.' "[21]

In Oregon, for example, the annual report of the Portland Radio Council (PRC) stated that its initial membership was 37 in 1940. The Portland Radio Council's goals were (1) to stress the importance of more discriminate radio listening, (2) to publicize radio programs of merit through radio guides and bulletins, (3) to publish information on "what is new in radio," and (4) to establish a speaker's bureau to provide speakers on the subject of "radio" at various meetings. The report noted, "The Portland Radio Council's war-time function is to continue to serve the listening public and act as an intermediary between community interests and the radio industry."[22]

One of the organization's accomplishments according to PRC's annual report, was a survey of children's and parents' attitudes toward radio. In May 1942, the PRC sent out a questionnaire to four Portland elementary schools and obtained the following data: children in the four schools average eight and one-half hours per week listening to radio, 300 respondents (parents) indicated they were not "completely satisfied with radio programs available to your child," but 269 answered that they were "completely satisfied."

The questionnaire also sought parents' attitudes regarding the types of radio programs and obtained the following data: "Disapproval of programs built around crime, horror, gun-play and those of 'cliff-hanger' variety;" and recommendations for more programs built on humor, music, Bible stories, children's activities, story telling, and dramatization of good children's books, history, and lives of famous men and women. "The committeee recommends that copies of the findings be sent to the commercial radio stations of this area."[23]

Since those NAB-supported councils were composed of both private individuals and representatives of various organizations, mainly women's clubs, Lewis' estimates of the total number of persons participating could be accurate. On the other hand, her figures could be interpreted as industry exaggeration. Thirty years later, in 1971, she noted, "60 Radio Councils statewide, areawide and/or citywide were functioning in the 1940s. Some still are operating but in a less dynamic way."[24]

WOMEN'S NATIONAL RADIO COMMITTEE

In addition to the number of radio councils Lewis helped establish, there was a parallel movement, which had been started earlier and was perhaps more extensive. The Women's National Radio Committee, founded in September 1934, by Yolanda Moroirion of New York, who claimed to have a "train of critical listeners from there to Catalina Island." Ralph Smith described the organization as "an amalgam of a score of women's clubs which singled out specific programs for brief statements in its monthly bulletin, Radio Review, of either commendation or castigation."[25] Forty thousand copies of the first issue were distributed free. Radio Review, published for at least two years, was supplemented by annual awards, which the Women's National Radio Committee bestowed on "deserving programs." The impetus for the committee's formation was a growing concern over "the effect of radio on young people. Women's groups in several communities undertook a pioneering job of monitoring programs, constructing criteria for their evaluation, and promoting those which were deemed worthwhile. This promotion took place primarily by working through the public schools."[26]

According to Business Week, "For more than six months, the Women's National Radio Committee has aggressively promoted its crusade for radio reforms, has rallied to its standard 10 million women, members of various organized women's groups."[27]

ASSESSMENT OF THE COUNCILS

Admittedly, it is difficult to determine the effectiveness of the councils regarding their relationships with the broadcasters since each group—the NAB-supported councils, the Women's National Radio Committeee, and the broadcasters—could inflate its sense of performance. Yet some indication of the attitudes and policies of some broadcasters exists, and the existence of numerous councils and committees at least implies that they did function to some extent. Also, the networks and the NAB did lend early support.

If Literary Digest and Business Week were accurate in their accounts of accomplishments of the Women's National Radio Committee, then the committee's effectiveness and relationships with the broadcasters and networks were indeed impressive. The committee's actions could well be used as examples or models for subsequent citizens' groups.

Literary Digest noted, "The Women's National Radio Committee is not interested in popularity polls or the comparative pulling powers of this or that program in terms of merchandise sold. It was founded with the express purpose of cleaning up certain self-evident abuses, and then holding the sponsors, broadcasting networks and entertainers in line by crusading against the objectionable and placing a premium on excellence."[28]

Business Week described the committee following the group's presentation of its second annual broadcast award meeting:

> The W.N.R.C. made good its threat to "name names"—and publish them against these programs, which still offend good taste, despite the broadcasting companies reform efforts. To advertising men who read the first six-page issue of Radio Review several pertinent facts about W.N.R.C. and its claimed membership of 10 million were readily apparent. First, the women were not given to euphemisms—as their castigations of the seven programs indicate . . . —second, they were not wholly dedicated to symphonic programs and educational broadcasts. Their first review spoke kindly of lighter box office attractions. . . . [29]

An earlier issue of Business Week stated,

> Radio executives have apparently concluded that 10 million women can't be wrong—especially when their judgements are substantially supported by the Chairman of the FCC. That is the deduction which advertisers and advertising agencies are drawing from the matter-of-fact statement they issued this Tuesday from the offices of CBS announcing that 1) that CBS would not accept any new laxative accounts, renew existing ones . . . or permit any broadcast which describes graphically or repellently any internal bodily functions, symptomatic results of internal disturbances or matters not considered

acceptable topics in social groups; 2) that it would
also ban all blood-and-thunder themes from juvenile
programs which were not acceptable to "an eminent
child psychologist" . . . .; 3) that it would not permit
after July 30, when the whole program goes into effect,
any commercial announcement which exceeded 10 percent
of the total broadcast time for an evening program or 15
percent of a day program, a special extra allowance of
40 seconds being made for quarter-hour programs. [30]

The Women's National Radio Committee was assisted by 27
cooperating organizations including the American Association of
University Women, the Association of the Junior League of America,
the General Federation of Women's Clubs, the Daughters of the
American Revolution, and the Women's Christian Temperance Union.
The committee's executive secretary told Literary Digest, "We want
more than anything to avoid being righteous, smug. We are earnest
women pioneering where the returns can only be in the form of satisfaction." And the Digest observed, "It is this tremendous cross-
sectional force which has heaped anathema on the blues sisters,
amateur hours, blood-and-thunder children's programs, and 'true
confessions' of the air."[31]

INDUSTRY'S REACTION

Regarding the broadcast industry's reaction to the councils,
Albert Williams stated, "The National Association of Broadcasters
is, of course, in complete sympathy with listener groups of this
nature. Such groups provide broadcasters with a set of checks and
balances that will guarantee full freedom of the air because of the
guarantee to the listener against inroads of his patience and privacy."[32]
NAB's interest was not motivated strictly by social responsibility.
Councils could also help the broadcasters by supporting certain programs—and sponsors.

The public's affection for radio is almost quaint. No
other medium arouses as much comment or such a
sense of personal possession. . . . Listeners should
help by buying products of those (wartime) sponsors
of good programs and of those merchandise they
approve. Today listeners, when vocal, should be
patient and considerate. [33]

This view was reinforced by a broadcaster at a Pacific north-west radio station working with a council in 1941. He indicated that his station used the council to help promote programs and sponsors; but he was quick to add that councils are not needed today. [34]

Following is an observation by a station manager of WMT in Cedar Rapids, Iowa, who made the remarks at a 1944 NAB meeting in Chicago:

Radio councils are simplifying the problems of public
service programs for broadcasters in many parts of
the country. Even more important, they provide broadcasters and community leaders an opportunity to exchange
viewpoints, something that is sadly lacking in altogether
too many localities. In Cedar Rapids we are demonstrating
that broadcasters and organizations can work together
harmoniously to the distinct advantage of the community
we serve. [35]

FCC SUPPORT

In addition to community and industry support, radio councils were also endorsed by the Federal Communications Commission:

Radio listener councils can also do much to improve
the quality of program service. Such councils, notably
in Cleveland, Ohio, and Madison, Wisconsin have already
shown the possibilities of independent listener organization.
First they can provide a much needed channel through which
listeners can convey to the broadcasters the wishes of the
vast but not generally articulate radio audience. Second,
listener councils can engage in much needed research concerning public tastes and attitudes. Third, listener councils can check on the failure of network affiliates to carry
outstanding network sustaining programs and on the local
programs. . . . Fourth, they can serve to publicize and
to promote outstanding programs—especially sustaining
programs which at present suffer a serious handicap for
lack of the vast promotional enterprise which goes to
publicize many commercial programs.

Other useful functions would also no doubt result from an
increase in the number and extension of the range of

activities of listener councils cooperating with the broadcasting industry but speaking solely for the interest of
listeners themselves. [36]

Of the estimated 60 councils, several were cited as exemplary:
The Rocky Mountain Council, the Minnesota Radio Council, and the
Cleveland Radio Council, which was mentioned by the FCC. A brief
examination of the Cleveland group—which still exists, will be offered
in Chapter 5, together with a description of other contemporary
citizens' groups.

WHY THE COUNCILS WERE FORMED

At this point, it might be helpful to examine briefly what factors
prompted the councils to come into existence. Were radio broadcasts
in bad taste? Did programming offend local audiences? Were there
advertising excesses? Was there a shortage of broadcast critics?
    As an indication of one attitude toward radio, the _Atlantic
Monthly_ stated in its January 1948 issue,

> Radio presents its sorriest spectacle in the daytime. The
> listener has a choice of soap opera, give-away shows, or
> quizzes which mean he may listen to the heart-rendering
> sobs of Helen Trent or squeals of rapture from the studio
> audience. . . . In its craze for listeners radio has become
> the most incestuous of all the arts. There is hardly a
> successful radio program which has not provoked a dozen
> scrofulous little imitations designed to look as nearly like
> the original as the laws of plagiarism will allow. [37]

The article also accused radio of overcommercialization, appealing
to mass audiences to please the advertisers, and of not using its
full potential for the public interest.
    The March 1947 issue of _Fortune_ stated, "The U.S. Radio
industry has persuasively demonstrated that the U.S. radio listeners
are not only willing but eager to accept the great part of broadcasting.
But does that excuse the U.S. radio for continuing to offer pretty
much the same old vaudeville in the same old way—to jam the air
with that sticky commodity. Many critics of radio say no. They say
it is no way to treat a public franchise. . . . In some U.S. cities
attempts have been made toward program improvement through the
formation of listeners' pressure groups." [38]

Another possible reason why citizens'councils were formed may
have been due to a lack of critics, professional as well as amateur.
Llewellyn White reported that

> Far more remarkable than the meagerness of (broad-
> casting) awards, however, is the dearth of praise and
> constructive criticism in the other media. . . . all
> newspapers and magazines except a half dozen on the
> order of Harper's, the Atlantic, the New Republic, and
> The Nation were "not interested." . . . A curious veil,
> half bitter jealousy and half studied indifference, sep-
> arates the general press from the newest medium of
> of information and entertainment. More newspaper
> space is devoted to the interests of bridge players and
> stamp collectors than to radio in all its aspects. Variety,
> in January, 1946, reported that of the 1,700 dailies, only
> 324 "pretend to employ" radio editors, and qualified only
> 45-50 for the title by the farthest stretch. The others
> were "mostly office boys or old men" who simply print
> daily radio logs, and now and then "highlighting" a few
> programs. Newspapers in San Francisco and Los Angeles
> have agreements forbidding them to use radio columns. [39]

Those observations were brought up to date by Jack Gould, New
York Times television critic, who observed,

> The American press by and large is giving television
> a dangerous and short-sighted free ride in its columns.
> It has surrendered to the easy and inexpensive policy of
> dishing fan magazine pap and ignoring the evolution of a
> cultural medium of unrivaled social force. If the quali-
> tative level of the entertainment of TV has shown relent-
> less deterioration, the press shares part of the respon-
> sibility. On the 1,650 newspapers there are not more
> than 10 critics who are paid to examine TV both esthet-
> ically and sociologically. The practical effect . . . is
> to let the TV junk go unprotested and leave the TV accom-
> plishment inadequately cheered and encouraged. . . . [40]

Admittedly, those magazines and the New York Times may not
represent the "average" listening or viewing public since those publications are generally regarded as "class" magazines read primarily
by the better educated. But there may have been some truth in their
assessment of broadcasting; otherwise the councils might not have
been organized.

WHY THE COUNCIL MOVEMENT DECLINED

Regarding the duration of the early councils' existence, such information is scarce. White offers a clue to some of the difficulties encountered by the councils:

> From the earliest days of broadcasting, loosely organized listener groups have clustered around local service and women's clubs, PTA associations, and energetic educators and clergymen. Few of them have clearly defined programs or goals; and those that have, have been fairly limited and specific about them: More "wholesome" children's programs, more "good" music, more in-school training, more Sunday morning time for sermons, and so on. As with most voluntary and quasi-social groups, the majority have found it difficult to sustain interest and even attendance at meetings. [41]

Hence it is conceivable that members were not motivated enough to participate.

And despite the national scope of the council activity, the movement began to decline shortly after World War II began. Its demise was expedited by the NAB in 1948 when that organization apparently reversed its policy of supporting the councils. When Lewis left her position as coordinator of listener activity, the NAB did not replace her, apparently terminating that position. She wrote, "When I joined the United Nations in 1948 no one was left at NAB to serve as liaison (for the councils). There were a few (4 or 5) on the National Board of NAB who feared that I was building a Frankenstein!"[42]

In addition to the lack of NAB support and the rise of World War II, several other reasons can be cited to help explain the decline of the radio council movement: (1) the lack of government support, (2) the rising popularity of television, (3) the membership composition of the councils, and (4) the apparent maturing and financial advances of the broadcasting industry to the extent that broadcasters felt they no longer needed citizen advice or help.

Concerning lack of government support, in 1940 Congress terminated the Educational Radio Project sponsored by the U.S. Office of Education. Within a year all funds for the Federal Forum Project were cut off. This signaled the end of federal financing in broadcasting, which started in the 1930s. [43]

Related to this is the second factor: the advancement of television, which was beginning to flower in the early 1940s when the second world war interrupted its progress. The war also helped divert public attention from broadcasting as an entertainment instrument to a vehicle to promote patriotism. As Dorothy Palmer, former president of the Minnesota Radio Council, wrote, "The Council took a back seat during World War II. I devoted my every working moment to that (effort)."[44]

The membership of the councils, in some cases, did not represent the whole of society—and this may have been their greatest weakness. Most councils were composed of group representatives of organizations such as the General Federation of Women's Clubs, the National PTA, the Junior League, or the National Council of Churches. Williams observed,

> For one thing, the organizations do not represent
> listeners. They represent listening church goers,
> listening club women, or listening parents. As such,
> their primary interest is the development of other
> matters than a radio system, and radio listening
> is only a partial means to a different end. [45]

The observation by Williams that membership in the early councils did not represent a cross section of American socioeconomic society was suggested in Chapter 1, which noted that citizen participation tends to increase with the amount of education of the individual. This view has been supported by Dale Rogers Marshall: "Studies of the relation of SES (Socio-economic-status) to participation all indicate that various social strata participate differently," and that all involvement in formal organizations is positively associated with such status. "Only the middle and upper-class tend to be associated with civic and service associations."[46] A study in 1958 by sociologist Charles Wright reported similar findings.[47]

Related to this were the profits made by stations during the war. Broadcast historian Erik Barnouw noted that, because of the newsprint shortage during the war, newspapers were forced to turn down advertising; and that worked to the benefit of radio stations. Also, because of the high excess-profits tax during the war, corporations spent money on advertising that otherwise would have been paid in taxes. "The avalanche of advertising that came to radio from 1941 on represented many advertisers with nothing to sell."[48]

Probably because of this "avalanche" the industry felt it had come of age and that it no longer needed to enlist or support groups to promote itself and its sponsors. One can also theorize that the growing influence of audience rating firms also may have had some influence on broadcasters—and on the advertisers. Simply stated, all those factors, highlighted by Lewis' resignation, provided the broadcast industry with a convenient rationale for not continuing its support of the council movement.

The loss of most of the early councils has not gone unnoticed.
Walter B. Emery, former FCC staff member and academician, wrote,

> Back in the forties, a movement for the development
> of listener councils got started. I was always sorry
> the movement did not get very far. It would be help-
> ful if it could be revived. Every community ought to
> have such a council, composed of thoughtful people
> with varied interests, conducting studies, and making
> evaluations of programs and passing them on to broad-
> casters for consideration. [49]

Although the councils substantially diminished, not all of them
disbanded. Others have been organized since World War II, and more
recent ones have emerged within the past decade. The new groups
appear mainly concerned with television, but radio has not been
neglected. It is to the formation and thrust of several different types
of citizens' groups that the following section will be directed.

THE RECENT MOVEMENT

Despite the dissolution of most of the early councils following
the outbreak of World War II, at least one such group continued to
exist, the Greater Cleveland Radio and Television Council. But in
general, only recently has there been a renewal of interest by
citizens' groups in broadcasting. As noted in Chapter 1, this re-
surgence could be considered an extension of the consumer movement
of the 1960s. A few groups, however, were organized between 1945
and the 1960s, such as the American Council for Better Broadcasting,
the National Association for Better Broadcasting, and the Wisconsin
Radio and Television Council.

In addition to those groups, a number of more recent community
organizations have been formed, such as the Chinese Media Committee, the Community Coalition for Media Change, both in San Francisco;
the Columbus (Ohio) Broadcasting Coalition, the Coalition for the
Enforcement of Quality in Television and Radio in New Mexico, and
others. [50] These newer groups have been formed since 1969 when the
United States Court of Appeals ruled in the WLBT (TV) Jackson,
Mississippi, case that members of the public have a first amendment
right of legal standing to challenge existing broadcast license renewals.
These groups have been supported by yet another type of citizens'
organization—legal resource and expertise centers such as the Stern
Community Fund, the United Church of Christ Communications Section,
and the Citizens Communications Center.

In 1955, the U.S. President's Council of Economic Advisors requested Consumer's Union to prepare a memorandum on the subject of "The Government Regulatory Agencies." Consumer's Union Report noted that the FCC was

> a demoralizing spectacle—a regulatory agency whose licensees are in frequent and blatant violation of federal law while the regulators, themselves, violate the very law they themselves have promulgated. . . . the thesis of this memorandum is, therefore, that only through the implementation of the consumer position in government can an avenue be opened up for the effective expression of the public interest in such regulatory programs as that administered by the FCC.[51]

In December 1960, following the television quiz show scandals, the FCC held hearings in Washington, D.C., at which the Consumer's Union representatives testified. The commission asked for opinions on television programming and for suggestions for improvements. In submitting a proposal, the consumer organization suggested the establishment of a "Television and Radio Consumers Council," which would act as an advisory unit to the FCC. The proposed council would (1) review all FCC licensing decisions, (2) request additional data on a licensee's performance, and (3) publicize its findings.[52]

The proposal also requested (1) mandatory hearings in all license renewals to be held in the locale of the broadcasting station; (2) publicity of the renewal hearings involved for a given number of days at fixed hours, inviting public participation in the proceedings; (3) requiring broadcasters to maintain for public investigation the commitments he made regarding programming and advertising; (4) requiring each broadcaster to air at least once a week during prime time "a statement of the basis upon which he holds the exclusive privilege to the public domain and invite set-owner comment on the station's programming and advertising and establish in each of the FCC's 24 district offices a consumer review staff to read and classify public responses and to forward such material to the Consumer Advisory Council of the FCC; (5) requiring the declarations of advertising policy to be posted for public inspection in each licensee's place of business; (6) prohibiting the sale of any license without a full scale rehearing on the transfer of the privilege; and (7) setting up a graduated system of licensing fees based on station signal-strength and on advertising revenues. The Consumer's Union also called for the "immediate revival and re-issuance" of the FCC's 1946 "Blue Book."[53]

Broadcasting, the broadcast industry's trade journal, marks the beginning of the citizen group activity at about the same period as the Consumer's Union report.

The history of citizen involvement in station-sale
proceedings goes back at least to 1961. Then it was
not merely a group but a state—New Jersey—that
opposed the sale of WNET TV New York [then the
commercially operated WNTA TV (Channel 13)] by
National Telefilm Associates to its present owner,
Educational Television for the Metropolitan Area,
on the ground that New Jersey would be deprived of
its only VHF (Channel 13 is still assigned to Newark).[54]

The FCC approved the sale, but New Jersey went to court, and Educational Television won a settlement by pledging to devote one hour
of news coverage daily to matters of interest to New Jersey.

Perhaps the first citizen group activity that occurred recently
was in 1963 when a citizens' group opposed the sale of KOVR (TV)
owned by Metromedia, Inc., in Sacramento, to the McClatchy Newspaper chain, which "had a monopoly of news."[55] The group registered
its opposition with its congressman, not with the FCC. The FCC
approved the sale. Over the following several years, there were a
few more unsuccessful efforts by citizens' groups involving opposition
to the sale of KARK AM-FM TV to Mullins Broadcasting Co., in
Little Rock, Arkansas, and the sale of WROK AM-FM TV, Rockford,
Illinois to WROK Inc. The FCC's actions "ended matters," and no
appeals resulted.[56]

RECENT CITIZENS' GROUP ACTIVITY

Broadcasting noted that it was not until a citizens' group in
Chicago in 1968 protested the sale of WFMT (FM) to the Tribune
Company's WGN Continental Broadcasting Company that citizens'
groups "discovered their muscle in such proceedings."[57] The United
States Court of Appeals in that case ruled that the FCC should have
given "detailed consideration to the group's protest, even though it
had filed late and in improper form. The court sent the case back
to the FCC for further proceedings." The court's decision was similar
to its 1969 ruling in the WLBT (TV) case, which generally was regarded as a landmark decision for citizens' groups. The FCC's
decision that the Boston Herald Traveler should surrender its WHDH-
TV license to a local group on the basis of diversification of media

in 1969 also has been cited as an example of citizens' group achieve-
ment.[58] There were, however, other factors involved in that complex
case.*

The more recent citizens' group activity seems to have common
characteristics: a concern about programming for racial minorities;
a concern about employment and training programs for women and
racial minorities; a concern about excessive or unethical advertising—
including advertising for children; a concern about absentee ownership of stations and a lack of local programming; and a desire to be
consulted by broadcasters concerning the ascertainment of community
problems and needs.

Perhaps the term "access" would be appropriate in attempting
to describe or synthesize those common traits: access to program
planning, access to the airwaves, access to helping establish employment practices, access to station management, legal access to challenge
license renewals. In describing the citizens' group movement, Broadcasting stated,

> The groups are rich in the diversity of America: blacks
> from the inner city, chicanos and Latinos from the barrios
> of the Southwest and West, Chinese from San Francisco's
> Chinatown, groomed WASP housewives from the suburbs
> and the big cities.
>
> All are angry and frustrated. Broadcasting is so persuasive
> it has become a personal thing to them; they would feel they
> had a claim on it even if they had never heard that the air-
> waves belong to the public. And they all have heard that.

---

*That station's problems began in 1947 when newspaper pub-
lisher Robert Choate obtained a temporary license from the FCC to
operate WHDH-TV. In the following 25 years, eight companies com-
peted for that license. There were six appeals to the Federal Circuit
Court, and four to the U.S. Supreme Court. One of the accusations
in the final hearing was that a previous FCC chairman, George
McConnaughey, admitted he had dined with Choate during a previous
hearing period. Another reason for the FCC's ruling was that the
Herald Traveler had shifted the station's executive control in 1963
without commission permission, and that the station's owners were
only slightly involved in daily management of the station.

Broadcasting, they would seem to feel, is letting them
down; it is not serving _their_ interests, reflecting _their_
needs, expressing _their_ points of view. [59]

The recent citizens' organizations appear to be community
groups with specific goals aimed at particular stations. And once
these goals are attained, the associations probably would disband or
become less active. That is to say, once the group has achieved
recognition and commitments from a radio or television station to
change certain policies or practices, the citizens' group would lose
its reason for existence. A few key leaders might continue to monitor
a station's programs to determine if the broadcaster were fulfilling
his pledge; and if the promise were not carried, the group could again
assert itself.

SUMMARY

There have been apparent similarities between the interests of
the early citizens' groups and the more recent ones. The Radio Council
on Children's Programs seemed just as concerned about adequate
programming for youngsters as Action for Children's Television,
although the former group was interested in radio.

The concept of having local citizens participate in groups involved
in broadcasting also struck a responsive point with the formation of
radio listening panels in cities across the nation. This concept was
encouraged by the National Association of Broadcasters, which actively
supported such groups. When the NAB ceased its support the citizens
movement substantially diminished; and, along with other factors, it
eventually reached a point where local groups were no longer effective,
if indeed they continued to exist at all.

The FCC also lost, for a while, interest in supporting citizens'
groups. Perhaps it was recovering from attacks the FCC received
after issuing the "Blue Book."* But in the late 1950s and early 1960s,

----

*_Public Service Responsibility of Broadcast Licensees_ (Wash-
ington, D. C.: Government Printing Office, 1946) is commonly referred
to as the "Blue Book," the color of the publication's cover. It criticized
the broadcast industry for excessive commercial practices and stations
for not performing what they promised to broadcast. The publication
and the FCC were attacked by the broadcast industry.

both the commission and the public again began to show a new interest in broadcasting—this time in television. Developments occurred that again encouraged the formation of citizens' groups.

The following chapter will discuss how the broadcast industry, has tended to react to the more recent groups, which can be divided into three general types. The local group has stability and seeks to work with broadcasters in an amicable relationship. This group tends to have as members representatives from local women's and civic and educational organizations. An example of this type would be the Greater Cleveland Radio and Television Council. The second type is a group that seeks national membership and tends to have an aggressive posture, not hesitating to petition or challenge local stations, the commercial networks, or the FCC. Such an example would be Action for Children's Television. The third type is the legal resource center, which offers legal expertise to other citizens'groups, such as the Citizens Communication Center (CCC). CCC has operated on a national basis and has been involved directly and indirectly in a number of cases in which citizens' groups have challenged or petitioned stations.

It should be noted that this grouping is arbitrary, other types of citizens' groups could be offered. For example, many more recent groups, as noted earlier, tend to be composed of racial minority groups with their own demands. This type has not been included because such groups seem to lack stability and staying power. This is not to say they have not been effective. Indeed some of them have been instrumental in effectuating change.

PRESS COUNCILS

A number of commissions, both private and public, have studied the mass communications system and have suggested the establishment of some form of advisory councils to the media—both on the community level and the national level. The 1946 Hutchins Commission on Freedom of the Press endorsed the organization of local councils, and the more recent President's Commission on the Causes and Prevention of Violence suggested the establishment of a national advisory organization.

Related to the concept of citizens' broadcast councils are press councils, which normally are regarded as applying more to newspapers and to the print media than to broadcast media. Yet a few radio and television stations are members of press councils, which tend to operate in the same manner as broadcast councils. These have been described by William Rivers, et al. in <u>Backtalk</u>.[60]

Other nations have also implemented some forms of media advisory councils. These include Sweden, Switzerland, England, West Germany, Turkey, Austria, Japan, South Africa, Canada, Israel, South Korea, India, The Philippines, and Indonesia.[61] In many of these countries, however, the councils apply to print media and not to broadcasting. The British Broadcasting Corporation does use citizens' panels, and the Nihon Hoso Kyokai (NHK) in Japan also uses advisory bodies.

A more recent organization established in the United States in 1973 is the National News Council. NNC was developed by the Twentieth Century Fund; and although not endorsed by all the news media, it will investigate legitimate complaints concerning both print and broadcast media. As of August 1974, it had received 250 complaints, 19 of which concerned radio and television, the rest involving other media. Forty-four ended in adjudication.[62]

In addition to press councils, there are precedents in other areas of mass communication in which citizens' groups have made an impact. Both the film industry and the comic book field have had experiences with local groups. The comic book industry was the object of attack by the National Organization for Decent Literature (NODL), which "initiated the techniques of blacklisting 'objectionable' comic books."[63]

The NODL was organized in 1938 by a council of Roman Catholic bishops to "develop a plan for organizing a systematic campaign in all dioceses of the United States against the publication and sale of lewd magazines and brochure literature." The group's "decency crusades" involved the Archdiocesan Council of Catholic Women and the General Federation of Women's Clubs, which also worked at the community level using local chapters to supress "objectionable" literature.[64]

Because of the extent of both national and community group criticism, by the mid-1950s comic book publishers organized the Comics Magazine Association of America to prevent possible congressional legislation and to stop a declining sales trend. The association adopted a Comics Code Authority to "keep all future comic books, regardless of type, up to recognized standards for decent, wholesome reading matter."[65]

Regarding the film industry, Jack Schwartz of the Institute of Communications Research at the University of Illinois, wrote, "Civic groups have been criticizing film content ever since 'The Widow Jones,' an 1896 film, was attacked for containing a kiss." In 1919 the General Federation of Women's Clubs voiced criticism of the film industry.[66]

A number of states and municipalities have had movie censorship boards since the turn of the century. Chicago had one in 1907, New York in 1909, Pennsylvania in 1911, and Kansas in 1913. Rivers, Theodore Petersen, and Jay Jensen wrote that censorship of the movies appears to have been tolerated for several reasons: first, movies were regarded primarily as entertainment and in their infancy were linked with vaudeville houses; second, excesses of the film industry during the post-World War I period created a climate of opinion favorable to restrictions; and third, producers "tried to outdo one another in luring the public with risque titles, lurid advertisements, and passionate love scenes."[67] (The first and third reasons conceivably could be applied to broadcasting. That is, some critics regard broadcasting as primarily an entertainment medium; and it seems obvious to state that broadcasters do indeed try to outdo one another in their search for larger audiences.)

There are two well-established organizations involved in film criticism: The National Catholic Office for Motion Pictures (NCOMP), formerly known as the National Legion of Decency, and the Film Estimate Board of National Organizations. The NCOMP, composed of Roman Catholic laymen and clergy, rates films on a regular basis and circulates the ratings to all dioceses and, to a limited extent, to the general public. These ratings are used as "moral guides" by church officials. "Decisions to implement the ratings through organized activity, and the choice of methods to be used, are left with the bishop in each diocese, and, to a lesser extent, with local priests."[68]

NCOMP's predecessor, the National Legion of Decency, was established in 1934 "out of exasperation with the American film industry." Richard Randall observed that the Roman Catholic Church "probably ranks as the most important single group in the control of movies in this country at any level: production, distribution, or exhibition."[69]

The second group concerned with the film industry is the Film Estimate Board of National Organizations. The board is composed of members from the American Jewish Committee, American Library Association, Federation of Motion Picture Councils, the National Congress of Parents and Teachers, National Federation of Music Clubs, National Society of Daughters of the American Revolution, Protestant Motion Picture Council, and the Schools Motion Picture Committee. The organization's expenses, including those of publication and distribution of the "Green Sheet," which evaluates current films, are underwritten by the Motion Picture Association of America (MPAA). The MPAA represents the major American film production and distribution companies. The "Green Sheet" is sent to the mass media, schools, libraries, churches, and other exhibitors.[70]

CITIZENS FOR DECENT LITERATURE

In addition to the above groups there is another type of citizens' organization concerned with the mass media: Citizens for Decent Literature (CDL). This organization was formed in 1956 by a Cincinnati, Ohio, corporation lawyer, Charles H. Keating, Jr.[71]

CDL was organized primarily to combat obscenity and smut. In 1965 CDL had a national mailing list of about 6,000 persons. "The group tried to attract active citizens who could not devote full time to the work; therefore, an effort is made to operate without a formal organization with a variety of time-consuming club chores."[72]

The organization's most active chapters were reported to be in Los Angeles, New York, Chicago, Hartford, and Dallas. There are from 50 to 100 CDL youth groups throughout the nation with 12 to 200 members each. CDL rents a 30-minute color film, "Perversion for Profit." CDL is also concerned with films, and in some communities local chapters are called Citizens for Decent Literature and Films.

The differences between CDL and NODL are in their methods. CDL officials have said CDL "seeks to get courts to punish pornographers and ban their works, and NODL decides by fiat what works are good or bad, without recourse to the courts and the people. Authority to make arbitrary decisions is the essential element in the kind of censorship that CDL is against."[73]

Critics of citizens' groups, press councils, citizens' coalitions, or other types of community organizations have claimed that such bodies would be a threat to the mass media. Such charges usually center around the accusation that local citizens' groups could become a "watch and ward society," or a local censoring vehicle.

Most of the citizens' groups involved with the film industry and with the area of comic books have been concerned primarily with the effect of those media on children. In answer to the criticism of censorship, Walter Lippmann wrote,[74]

> Censorship is no doubt a clumsy and usually a stupid
> and self-defeated remedy. . . . But a continual ex-
> posure of a generation to the commercial exploitation
> of the enjoyment of violence and cruelty is one way to
> corrode the foundations of a civilized society. For my
> part, believing as I do in freedom of speech and thought,
> I see no objections in principle to censorship of the mass
> entertainment of the young. Until some more refined way
> is worked out for controlling this evil thing, the risks to
> our liberties are, I believe, decidedly less than the risks
> of unmanageable violence.

Conceivably, local citizens' groups could become community censoring boards. But the experiences of the early radio councils such as the Greater Cleveland Radio and Television Council have indicated otherwise.

NOTES

1. Ralph L. Smith, "A Study of The Professional Criticism of Broadcasting in the United States, 1920-1955" (unpublished Ph.D dissertation, University of Wisconsin, 1959), p. 34.

2. Judith Waller, Radio, The Fifth Estate (Boston: Houghton-Mifflin, 1950), p. 309.

3. Smith, op. cit., p. 35.

4. Arthur Jacoby and Nicholas Babchuck, "Instrumental and Expressive Voluntary Associations," Sociology and Social Research 27 (July 1963): 213.

5. Richard Gale, "Social Behavior, Natural Resources and The Environment," (unpublished manuscript pending at Harper & Row, 1972), p. 9.

6. Gabriel Almond and Sidney Verba, The Civic Culture (Princeton: Princeton University Press, 1963), p. 300.

7. Ibid., p. 301.

8. Elliot Krause, "Functions of a Bureaucratic Ideology: Citizen Participation," Social Problems 26, No. 2 (fall 1968): 129.

9. The Center For The Study of Democratic Institutions, Bureaucracy and The Forests (Santa Barbara: The Center For The Study of Democratic Institutions, 1962), p. 13.

10. Herbert Gans, "The New Egalitarianism," Saturday Review, May 6, 1972, p. 46.

11. Robert Sigal, "Citizens Committees-Advice vs. Consent," Transaction 4, No. 6 (May 1967): 48.

12. Krause, op. cit.

13. Charles Siepmann, Radio, Television and Society (New York: Oxford University Press, 1950), p. 77.

14. Waller, op. cit., pp. 310-311.

15. John Ohliger, "The Listening Group," Journal of Broadcasting 13, No. 2 (spring 1969): 154.

16. Ibid.

17. Frank E. Hill and W. E. Williams, Radio's Listening Groups: The United States and Great Britain (New York: Columbia University Pres, 1941), p. 24.

18. Ohliger, op. cit.

19. Waller, op. cit., p. 309.

20. Dorothy Lewis, "Listener's Stake in American Radio," Broadcasting, July 13, 1942, p. 66.

21. Dorothy Lewis, Radio and Public Service, A Guide Book For Radio Chairmen (New York: The National Association of Broadcasters, 1944), p. 43.

22. Portland, Oregon, Radio Council, Annual Report (Portland: Portland Radio Council, 1943).

23. Ibid.

24. Letter to author from Dorothy Lewis, January 27, 1971.

25. Smith, op. cit., p. 29.

26. Ibid., p. 34.

27. "Cleaning Up Radio," Business Week, May 18, 1935, p. 25.

28. "Cluster of Awards for Programs," Literary Digest, May 2, 1936, p. 34.

29. "Radio Critics," Business Week, August 10, 1935, p. 23.

30. Business Week, May 18, 1935, op. cit.

31. Literary Digest, May 2, 1936, op. cit.

32. Albert N. Williams, Listening: A Collection of Critical Articles (Denver: University of Colorado Press, 1948), p. 127.

33. Dorothy Lewis, Broadcasting, op. cit.

34. Luke Roberts, former KOIN AM-FM TV public service director, private interview held in Portland, Oregon, February 15, 1971.

35. Waller, op. cit., p. 311.

36. Public Service Responsibility of Broadcast Licensees, Report of the Federal Communications Commission, 1946, in Documents of American Broadcasting, Frank J. Kahn ed. (New York: Appleton-Century-Crofts, 1968), p. 197-198.

37. John Crosby, "Radio and Who Makes It," Atlantic Monthly No. 1 (January 1948), p. 24.

38. "The Revolt Against Radio," Fortune No. 3 (March 1947), p. 175.

39. Llewellyn White, The American Radio, A Report on The Broadcasting Industry in The United States (Chicago: University of Chicago Press, 1947), p. 114.

40. Robert Summers and Harrison Summers, Broadcasting and The Public (Belmont, California: Wadsworth Publishing Co., 1967), p. 378.

41. White, op. cit., p. 113.

42. Lewis, January 27, 1971, letter to author.

43. Ohliger, op. cit., p. 36.

44. Letter from Dorothy Palmer, February 17, 1971.

45. Williams, op. cit., p. 123.

46. Dale Rodgers, "Who Participates in What," Urban Affairs Quarterly 4, No. 2 (December 1968): 204-5.

47. Charles Wright, "Voluntary Association Memberships of American Adults: Evidence From National Sample Surveys," American Sociological Review 23, No. 3 (June 1958): 286.

48. Erik Barnouw, The Golden Web (New York: Oxford University Press, 1968), pp. 165-6.

49. Walter Emergy, "Broadcasting Rights and Responsibilities in Democratic Society", The Centennial Review of Arts & Letters, III (Michigan State University: East Lansing, Michigan, 1964), p. 320.

50. "The Struggle Over Broadcast Access," Broadcasting, September 20, 1971, pp. 32-43.

51. "Where May We Ask, Was The FCC," Consumer Reports 25, No. 1 (January 1960): 9-11.

52. "Here, We Would Suggest, Is a Program for the FCC," Consumer Reports 25, No. 2 (February 1960): 93-5.

53. Ibid.

54. "Any Ceiling Now in Sight on The Price of Settling Sale Protests," Broadcasting, May 29, 1972, p. 19.

55. Ibid.

56. Ibid.

57. Ibid, p. 20.

58. Nicholas Johnson, How To Talk Back To Your Television Set (New York: Bantam Books, 1970), p. 201.

59. "The Struggle Over Broadcast Access," Broadcasting, September 20, 1971, p. 32.

60. William Rivers, William Blankenburg, Kenneth Stark, and Earl Reeves, Backtalk: Press Councils in America (San Francisco: Canfield Press, 1972).

61. Ralph L. Lowenstein, "Has AEJ Proved the Case for a National Press Council?", paper presented to Association for Education in Journalism, University of California, Berkeley, California, August 25, 1969.

62. William B. Arthur, executive director of the National News Council, paper presented at Association for Education in Journalism, University of California, San Diego, California, August 20, 1974.

63. Otto N. Larsen, Violence and the Mass Media (New York: Harper & Row, 1968), p. 178.

64. Ibid., p. 179.

65. Ibid., p. 244.

66. Ibid., p. 191.

67. William Rivers, Theodore Peterson, and Jay Jensen, The Mass Media and Modern Society (San Francisco: Rinehart Press, 1971), p. 155.

68. Richard Randall, Censorship of The Movies (Madison: University of Wisconsin Press, 1968), p. 160.

69. Ibid., p. 186.

70. Ibid., p. 186.

71. Edwin A. Roberts, The Smut Rakers, (Silver Spring, Md.: Newsbook, The National Observer, 1966), p. 100.

72. Ibid., p. 102.
73. Ibid., p. 111.
74. Quoted in Larsen, op. cit., p. 175.

3

REACTIONS OF
BROADCASTERS AND
CONGRESS TO
CITIZENS'
ORGANIZATIONS

To examine the attitudes and the reactions of the broadcast industry leaders in relation to the citizen council movement is admittedly difficult. There are 711 commercial television stations and more than 7,000 AM and FM radio stations, each with its own set of problems and outlooks. And not all broadcasters are members of the NAB. It is possible, however, that there are some common traits and attitudes that many broadcasters share.

This chapter will examine how some of the leaders in the broadcasting industry view the citizens' movement. It also will probe the NAB's policies regarding citizens' groups and determine if broadcasters, as a group, have similar and possibly shared attitudes and, if so, to examine their nature. Chapter 4 will examine how the FCC, the individual commissioners, the courts, and other agencies view citizens' groups.

As previously noted, the NAB did support early radio and listening councils. Indeed the NAB, as most trade associations, always has been interested in promoting public relations and has worked with citizens' groups of various kinds. It publishes a number of explanatory pamphlets and materials and offers a source of industry information. One of these publications is the Study Guide on Broadcasting, designed for community groups and classroom study. The 20-page booklet has been published in conjunction with the General Federation of Women's Clubs as "a study guide by its local women's clubs throughout the U.S."[1]

Early NAB support of the councils, however, was terminated in 1948 when Dorothy Lewis left as coordinator of listener activity, and the NAB did not replace her. As noted previously, there were a few NAB national board members who feared that she was creating a "Frankenstein."[2] Apparently some NAB board members felt the councils might grow to the point where they could become unmanageable.

Concerning NAB policy, Roy Danish, director of NAB's Television Information Office, wrote that the organization "does not have a policy on advisory councils. Situations differ so markedly from place to place that I have not been able to satisfy myself that councils are more than occasionally useful."[3]

In the area of license renewal challenges by current citizens' groups, the NAB stated in a petition to the FCC, "It would be myopic to assume that citizen participation will stop with a few minority groups and the women's liberation movement if there are advantages to be gained. The Commission is dealing with merely the tip of the iceberg. . . . Homosexuals have entered the area in California. Every national origin or ethnic group in the country is a potential petitioner."[4]

Indicating its concern about citizen participation, the NAB in 1972 analyzed the petitions filed with the FCC to deny license renewals. The analysis revealed that 75 percent of the petitions were based on employment discrimination, failure to ascertain community needs, or failure of programming for minorities. The remaining petitions were based on accusations of specific FCC violations. The NAB also noted that many of the petitions were "virtually identical," even though they were against varying stations in different markets.

Following is how the NAB characterized citizens' groups that have filed petitions:

> Stations were largely at the mercy of petitioners who worked their little blackmail game with increasing dexterity. . . . With few exceptions citizens groups have capitalized on the use, or threatened use, of the petition to deny, to wrest control of programming from stations, dictate employment quotas, force the naming of selected individuals to stations' boards of directors, obtain free advertising for minority businesses, and a host of other concessions in areas which are the sole province of the licensee.[5]

VIEWS OF NETWORK EXECUTIVES

Not all networks cooperated in the preparation of this investigation. Robert D. Kasmire, vice president of corporate information at NBC, wrote, "Mr. (Julian) Goodman and other NBC executives receive many similar requests for assistance on research projects. Proper responses would entail extensive time and careful attention, seriously cutting into their other responsibilities. For this reason we have had to adopt a policy of declining all such inquiries."[6]

More cooperation was received at the other networks. J. T. Hoover, manager of audience information at American Broadcasting Companies, (ABC) replied,

> We are cognizant of the existence of such groups and we are responsive to suggestions and comments from them. Naturally, some are more organized than others and some are more broadcast-oriented, as well. These groups range from informal church groups to larger organizations.

> We can only guess as to why radio councils died out. One reason might well be that radio has become a responsible news medium and more sophisticated and attuned to the public consciousness. Furthermore, there was a war that needed attention of these groups.

> We don't have a policy concerning television viewing groups. Some serve a constructive purpose and possibly fulfill a need. Others do not.

> ABC has a Board of Governors composed of general managers of our affiliate stations. In addition, of course, we maintain our Department of Broadcast Standards and Practices, which reviews all entertainment material before it is seen on this network.[7]

Concerning general network response, ABC appears to be the most vocal. Elton H. Rule, ABC president, in a speech in California in January 1972, stated,

> For our part, we will have to make every attempt to listen and to understand the language of those who approach our doors. For some of what we hear will be worth knowing, and will deserve creative response.

> By the same token, our ears are going to hear some vituperation, accusation and even curses. But ear plugs are no answer. They screen out all sound. We do not want to see repeated jaw-to-jaw confrontations, like the climatic scenes in an endless Western.

> We do want to see a meeting of the minds, a free exchange of ideas, an interaction of audience and broadcasters that results in better radio, better television.

> . . . Broadcasting is a very human industry. . . . If,
> in meeting the day-to-day demands of our profession,
> some among us have neglected to keep in close touch
> with the special needs of special segments of our
> audiences, it is time we corrected that error. [8]

In the same speech, Rule cited some experiences ABC-owned and operated stations have encountered with citizens' groups, and how the stations responded. The ABC television affiliate in Chicago, after a group filed a petition against it, had "frank and productive" meetings with members of the group. "The station telecasts programs with special relevance to minority problems. One result—the petition was withdrawn. Another—the station has a stronger sense of local identity." In San Francisco, the Chinese Media Committee "taught us something of the needs of the Chinese community," and KGO-TV "will soon experiment with an early morning program in Cantonese" to serve oriental viewers. Rule did not specify when the "experiment" would begin nor how it would operate. And his pledge to make every attempt to listen and understand does appear to be overly generous.

In Los Angeles, Rule continued, two citizens' organizations representing Mexican-Americans, Justicia and Nosotros, "came to ABC in a mood that can be described as angry. We sat down with the leaders of these groups and experienced a rewarding meeting of the minds." Rule described the meetings as a "sensitivity session, with no holds barred."

> First we talked, then they talked. We learned something
> of how the Mexican-American sees the world and especially
> the world of radio and television. They learned something
> of our problems and concerns. We sat together and watched
> some typical films and programs that had caused violent
> objection. After our discussions, with a changed outlook,
> we were able to see clearly the basis for some objection.
> And we agreed. On the other side, Justicia and Nosotros
> spokesmen saw occasions where their objection was not
> justified, but was simply based on hyper-sensitivity, and
> they recognized that fact.
>
> Our industry has called for legislation to clarify the
> ground rules relating to our very right to hold broad-
> cast licenses. The reason we seek this legislation is
> not because we want a wall to hide behind but because

we need a buffer against the winds of planned harrass-
ment that blow from so many directions. . . . It is
ABC's position that the FCC already has the power to
renew a station's license given evidence of that station's
responsible performance, and to protect that station
from petition or challenge.[9]

A director of community relations was hired for KABC-TV in
Los Angeles, as well as in Chicago and New York; and the ABC net-
work arranged frequent meetings with minority representatives. The
ABC president noted that his network strongly supports the "NAB
Bill" sponsored by Senator Stewart Moss of Utah and the one by
Congressman James Broyhill of North Carolina.[10]

The CBS network appears to value public criticism—but only of
a broad, general nature. In 1960, Frank Stanton, president of CBS,
said, "We owe it to our audience as well as to ourselves to try to
establish some systematic method of inviting the public to participate
in shaping what we do."[11] And in 1971, Leonard Spinrad, director of
corporate information at CBS, wrote,

More than 2,000 publications, for example, cover some
phase of television. Private and public organizations review and comment on what is presented on the air. The
CBS Television Network screens broadcasts in advance via
closed circuit for press reviewers across the country, so
that their reviews can appear in advance of broadcast.

Broadcasters are subject to the most powerful mechanism
in the world, the human thumb and forefinger that turns
the dial and switch the receiving set on and off. This,
of course, is the world's largest viewers' council. It
is our constant effort to be responsive to the needs and
interests of this vast public.[12]

Les Brown, Variety editor, noted that the "voting-with-the-dial"
concept in broadcasting, which is said to reflect the will of the viewing
majority as a "cultural democracy," is a myth. "More aptly, in the
area of entertainment, mainly it is a cultural oligarchy, ruled by a
consensus of the advertising community."[13] And Sydney Head, broadcasting academician, termed that concept as "simplistic," which "ig-
nores the rights of minorities."[14]

One CBS executive, Richard W. Jencks, then president of CBS
Broadcast Group and later CBS vice president, did offer his network's
views regarding community groups. In a speech entitled, "Broadcast
Regulation by Private Contract: Some Observations on 'Community
Control' of Broadcasting," Jencks noted that the consumer movement
in broadcasting had

stimulated regulatory action in a number of areas, of
which one of the most notable was in connection with
the broadcast advertising of cigarettes.

Consumerism is responsible for another development
in the broadcast field in which its role is quite different—
in which it seeks not so much to encourage regulatory
action as to substitute for government regulation a novel
kind of private regulation. [He noted that the idea of
community control of broadcasting] essentially got its
start in Jackson, Mississippi. . . . This decision gave
great impetus to the movement for citizen activism in
challenging the licenses of television and radio stations.[15]

Jencks appeared generally to be critical of community groups
and described most of them as having strong threads of "racial
separatism and puritanism" in their demands to stations. He noted
that originally community groups were black organizations in the
south and implied that most still are, or involve oriental or Chicano
racial members. He described, without naming, one group opposed
to entertainment programming. Jencks said this amounted to puritanism.
      The CBS executive observed that citizens' group demands to
broadcast stations raised a basic question "as to the purpose of a mass
medium in a democratic society. Should the broadcast medium be
used as a way of binding its audience together through programming
which cuts across racial and cultural lines? Or should it be used as
a means of communicating separately with differentiated segments of
its audience?" He noted that citizens' group challenges further "challenge the adequacy of the entire American system of broadcasting."
Jencks pointed out that television

can be said to be the only remaining mass medium which
is capable of reaching most of the people most of the time.
Is it important to preserve television as a mass medium?
I think so. . . . For the importance of television as a
mass medium has not been in what has been communicated
to minorities as such—or what has been communicated
between minority group leaders and their followers—but
in what has been communicated about minorities to the
general public.[16]

The network executive said he was opposed to community group
demands because their basic objectives would involve "the fragmenta-
tion of programming to serve what are perceived as ethnically relevant

interests." He also opposed them since such groups essentially would police a broadcast licensee "by means of exploiting the power of that very regulatory agency which is said to be 'unable or unwilling' to do so." He also observed that the demands community groups make on a station "are rarely, if ever, concerned with any constituents other than their own." Another reason he opposed them is that "private law enforcement is hard to control."

"A medium which can be coerced by threat of license contest into making such concessions to Black or Spanish-speaking groups can as readily be coerced by a coalition of white ethnic groups," Jencks stated. He also noted community groups are "loosely organized and tiny in membership. Not infrequently, the active members of a group seeking to contract with stations in a city of several million number scarcely more than a few dozen."

> So far the effectiveness of community group strategy has rested upon the willingness of the Commission to tacitly support these groups and their objectives. Indeed, it might well be argued that where the groups are successful in obtaining concessions, they can really be called government action. [17]

Jencks suggested that instead of encouraging community groups, the FCC should assume a more active stance.

> I would not be one to wish to encourage additional Commission regulation. But if there is more that the Commission feels it should do that it is not doing, I suggest it would be far more in the public interest for the Commission to do these things rather than to permit them to be done covertly by private groups.

> This does not mean that community groups have no proper role. There remains ample scope for community groups to press both broadcast licensees and the Commission for changes and improvements in American broadcasting, without turning over the job of regulation to such groups. [18]

CURRENT NAB RESPONSE TO CITIZENS' GROUPS

The number of television and radio stations that have been the objects of petitions filed with the FCC to deny the renewal of about 100 broadcast licensees is too large to allow an examination of the issues and participants. Indeed, the number appears to be steadily increasing. Each issue of Broadcasting seems to carry articles of stations affected by petitions. Many of the earlier license renewal cases have been described in former FCC Commissioner Nicholas Johnson's book, How to Talk Back to Your Television Set[19] and in special articles in Broadcasting.[20]

This section examines the public statements made by broadcast leaders and the industry and some of their public activities concerning the recent citizens' movement.

When Action for Children's Television (ACT) first presented its petition to the FCC asking that advertising for children be banned, the NAB stated in October 1971, that the elimination of advertising would sound the "death knell for quality children's program fare." In a formal comment filed with the FCC, the NAB accused the group of "painting an unfair and inaccurate picture" of American television. The NAB further argued that ACT was asking the television industry to offer children's programs at its own expense and had not proposed alternative means of financing such programs. "Such a proposal is unworkable, inequitable and without precedent."[21]

The following month, Roy Danish, director of the Television Information Office (TIO), commented on the ACT proposal that the networks devote two hours daily to commercial-free programs for children.

> We are being asked to move from the field of com-
> mercial broadcasting and to sustain the full costs
> of specifically and narrowly defined non-commercial,
> educational programming, while at the same time we
> forego the prospect of revenue for a substantial portion
> of each day. In addition, it is proposed that we be "en-
> couraged" to improve the quality of children's programs. . . .
> If the ACT proposal is rejected, the revenues attracted
> by the programs children will like will pay for the losses
> of the failures.*

---

*Presumably, Danish employed the term "failures" in the sense that such programs would not attract audiences large enough to attract advertisers and that such programs would not be profitable. A successful program would be just the opposite, drawing large audiences and advertisers.

Danish noted that the NAB fears the "tendency toward regulation which would force us to give away so much air-time that we could no longer function as a commercial medium."[22] Danish noted that the key issue in ACT's proposal was

> The demand that government formally mandate the
> number of hours that are to be programmed for a
> special category of viewers, in this case, children.
> But why not mandate additional hours to serve the
> special needs of other large and apparently homo-
> geneous groups? Why not for certain ethnic groups,
> or the elderly, or for religious and charitable move-
> ments which can claim a wide membership, or for
> political parties? . . . . Can we give each an hour
> of prime-time programming? Of course not. Not if
> there is to be an economic base to support the general
> entertainment and information programming that
> prompted viewers to buy their sets in the first place.[23]

However, the Code Authority of the NAB, at the suggestion of ABC, did adopt new policies regarding advertising for children. And the FCC in 1974 adopted new guidelines (not regulations) regarding programming for children. Indeed, after FCC Chairman Richard E. Wiley warned in May 1974 that the FCC would adopt its own remedies for problems in children's programming, the NAB acted one month later. The NAB ratified its code review board's set of recommenda-tions restricting both advertising time and the content of children's programming. Nonprogram time on Saturday and Sunday children's programs will be reduced to nine and a half minutes in 1976 on a graduated basis. Weekday nonprogram time will be limited to 14 minutes an hour in 1975 and 12 minutes in 1976. Several weeks later the Association of Independent Television Stations adopted similar rules for children's programs and advertising.[24]

Following is how Stockton Helffrich, director of the NAB Code Authority, viewed citizens' groups, including ACT:

> . . . the Code Authority, paralleling the position of
> responsible commercial broadcasters generally,
> believes that groups of the type you reference can
> serve a useful function both for broadcasters and
> their audiences. Our general policy includes sensi-
> tivity to whatever appeared to be valid expectations
> of broadcasters and broadcast materials (in program-
> ming and in advertising) affecting the public interest.

Challenges (to the Code Authority) generally appears to
be made up of a combination of unsolicited audience
opinion, competitors in given areas, medical and
scientific viewpoints, broadcasters' own insights,
etc. Any combination of these can and frequently
does result in Code Authority staff summations for
our Television Code Review Board or our Radio Board
(or both), sometimes with Code Authority recommendations and routinely appropriate Code Board discussion
and decision. [25]

In brief, the NAB's Code Authority appears in theory to be open
minded toward citizens' groups, but only after such groups vigorously
and vociferously have expressed their needs. The Code Authority also
appears to rely on a number of inputs for suggestions, but such sources
seem to emanate mainly from broadcasters—such as competition,
"broadcasters' own insights, etc." Helffrich's statement that the
NAB's policy of sensitivity to "whatever appears to be valid expecta-
tions of broadcasters and broadcast materials" was a very broad,
general statement offering wide latitude for interpretation by broadcasters. A cynic could interpret that policy as meaning "the public
interest is what the broadcasters say it is." An optimist could interpret it in an opposite manner.

REACTIONS TO LICENSE RENEWAL CHALLENGES

The possibility of a broadcast licensee facing license renewal
challenges appears to be a major concern of the industry. In 1971
Danish stated,

Today no licensee, regardless of how conscientiously
he has served his community, can approach license
renewal time with complete confidence. Instead, he
may find himself in contest with special interest groups
who want to strip him of his license for any of a growing
number of reasons. These range from allegations of unfair hiring practices and criticisms of program schedules
to demands for program control by non-broadcasters who
often represent only a handful of dissenters. . . . And as
the FCC wrestles with the renewal problem once again,
what is the position of the licensee? Should he make long-
term commitments for needed physical facilities? Is he
best advised to try to drain maximum profits during his
three-year term and then take his much diminished chances

to get a renewal? Should he change his promises at
each renewal date to please the tastes of a constantly
changing FCC?[26]

The spokesman for NAB noted that what the television broadcaster

requires most is elbow room to make the judgements
his experience dictates. . . . Just how each broadcaster will accommodate himself to the need for
change is, of course, unpredictable. But inevitably,
both at the network and local levels, resources available for programming will shrink and the net result
cannot help but be reflected in diminished service to
viewers.[27]

Danish's use of the term "inevitably" had a pessimistic ring
to it. This was compounded when he stated that resources would
shrink and service would be diminished. He seemed to be employing
an "either-or" type of rhetoric that implied either the broadcast
industry keeps the status quo, possibly lengthening license renewal
periods, or the system will shatter. He made no reference to com-
promises, or how broadcasters have learned of minority groups'
broadcast needs, or how broadcast service has improved. In brief,
his observation was a polemical statement.

LEGISLATIVE PROPOSALS

In his speech before the Poor Richard Club, Danish suggested
that the hope for broadcasters lies with the U.S. Congress.

It was in Congress that the words "interest, convenience
and necessity" were written to describe the basic elements in proper broadcast services. And we must look
to that body for recognition of a simple principle: good
performance, promised and delivered, should be rewarded
with renewal.[28]

Several congressmen who were apparently sympathetic to the
broadcast industry submitted a number of bills for legislation, which,
if adopted, would have offered the broadcaster more protection from
license renewal challenges. In 1969, Senator John O. Pastore
(Democrat, Rhode Island), chairman of the Senate Communications

Subcommittee, introduced Senate Bill 20004 to "stabilize the situation." Under the proposed legislation, the FCC could not consider a competing application for a license unless it had first taken the license away from the applicant for renewal."[29] Pastore noted at the time, "A person who has a license has to live up to the law, and when he does, and does a good job, he hadn't ought to be harrassed by an entrepreneur who comes in and makes a big promise." The bill was not successful, and Pastore apparently declined to again sponsor it. Former FCC Commissioner Nicholas Johnson at the time said Senate Bill 20004 would "counteract much of this wave of citizens' participation by prohibiting the filing of competing applications for existing radio and television stations."[30]

In October 1971, Senator John G. Tower (Republican of Texas) introduced a bill to give broadcast licensees additional protection against competing applications for their facilities. Senate Bill 2664 would have amended the Communications Act to provide that when there were mutually exclusive applications for a television or radio station to serve the same community, the FCC must first determine which of the applicants meets all of the basic qualifications required of a license such as financing, engineering, construction plans, and so forth. The bill also proposed that when one of the applicants is applying for renewal, his past record is to be considered by the FCC as being the best gauge of his future performance. New applicants would have been required to prove they could offer substantially better service than the incumbent before a station's license renewal could be denied.[31]

Tower's bill was similar to one introduced in the House of Representatives by Representative James T. Broyhill (Republican of North Carolina) earlier in 1971. That bill proposed to extend the licensing period from three to five years. Representative James Collins (Republican of Texas) said he believed Congress could be counted on to enact "legislation of the Broyhill bill (H.R. 539) if broadcasters can muster about 150 members of the House to become co-sponsors of the measure." However, former FCC Commissioner Lee Loevinger, Wendell Mayes, Jr., vice chairman of the Board of NAB, and Sol Taishoff, editor of Broadcasting, all noted that passage of the Broyhill measure would "not come easily." They cited the inevitable opposition of so-called "public interest and citizens' groups."[32]

In early 1972, more bills were introduced. Six bills, most of which carried similar proposals, were introduced in the House of Representatives. The sponsors were Virginia Representatives Watkins Abbitt and W. C. Daniel, James Kee (West Virginia), Thomas Morgan (Pennsylvania), Teno Roncalio (Wyoming), Robert Sikes (Florida), and Gus Yatron (Pennsylvania).[33]

Senator Richard S. Schweiker (Republican of Pennsylvania) introduced in April 1972, a bill to amend the Communications Act to provide that performance of an existing licensee will be a primary factor for the FCC to consider in license renewal proceedings. It would have extended the licensing periods for both radio and television stations from three to five years. [34]

In July, 1972, Congressman Fred B. Rooney (Democrat of Pennsylvania) said nearly 200 members of Congress in both houses and in both parties had lent their names to legislation regarding license renewal legislation. Rooney, who introduced a measure that would have extended the license period to five years for radio stations and retained the three-year period for television stations, urged broadcasters to "use the months to educate their congressmen as to the need for this legislation."[35]

Finally, in fall 1974, both the House and the Senate passed a measure to extend the broadcast license renewal period to five years. Although the final details had not been worked out and the measure had yet to be approved by a conference between the two houses, Broadcasting described passage of the bill as a "major victory for broadcasters." By a vote of 69 to 2, the Senate amended the Senate Commerce Committee's recommendation to retain the three-year renewal provision. [36]

In addition to extending the license period, the Senate bill provides the following: (1) directs the FCC at renewal time to consider if a licensee has followed the applicable ascertainment procedures, to consider if the licensee substantially has met the ascertained problems, needs, and interests, and if the station's operation was not "otherwise characterized by serious deficiencies;" the FCC shall grant a "presumption" in favor of the renewal if the applicant has satisfied the aforementioned three requirements; (2) it directs the commission to provide a rule establishing procedures for broadcast licensees to ascertain the needs, problems, and interests of their service areas; it directs the commission to determine how present regulations, which no longer serve the public interest, might be eliminated; and (3) it directs the FCC to finalize its multiple ownership rulemaking by the end of 1974. [37]

According to Broadcasting, Pastore explained to the Senate that the Commerce Committee had left the three-year renewal term in to "avoid weakening the impact of the petition to deny, used by minority and consumer groups at renewal time as a bargaining tool to gain access to a station's programming and hiring. I beg my colleagues today—do not remove the voice of the public . . . and compel it to wait five years before it can make a complaint," the Senator implored the Senate.

Senator John Tunney (Republican of California) who introduced
the five-year amendment, said he offered the measure for four reasons:
(1) it would reduce the commission's yearly renewal application work-
load by about 40 percent, which would allow the FCC to study applications more closely; (2) it would ease the burden of small broadcasters
for whom the renewal procedures are progressively complicated and
costly; (3) it would create an "improved climate for capital expenditures, allowing the broadcasters to amortize, over a reasonable
length of time, the heavy capital commitments necessary" to upgrade
their operations; and (4) it would enable the FCC to provide closer
scrutiny, which would assure the public that broadcasters are being
required to tailor their programming to serve community needs.[38]

The final House-Senate conference version, which broadcasters
hoped would be on the president's desk before Congress adjourned in
1974, did not make it, and the measure died.

Given the number of bills that have been proposed in both houses
during the recent years, it would not be surprising that broadcasters
and the NAB have achieved their goal. The relationship between Congress, the NAB, and the FCC at times has been very close. And
Tunney's observation that extending the license period from three
to five years would help relieve the FCC's workload does have some
merit.

OTHER NAB ACTIVITIES

The NAB also requested the FCC to divulge to broadcast
licensees the names of parties that have examined the commission's
public files concerning the stations.

The NAB general counsel, John Summers, in a letter to the
FCC sought clarification of commission procedures concerning public
examination of the agency's files. According to Broadcasting, Summers
in 1972 said, "It is difficult to understand why the licensee would
be denied access to the very information required to carry out such
an early dialogue—the names of those who have inspected the public
files relative to his station." His request noted that since the licensee
was aware of the identities of persons examining the local files, "why
should he be denied access to this same type of information where
the same files are inspected at the Commission instead of at the
station?" Summers said the NAB understands that the FCC employees
maintaining public files have been instructed not to reveal the identities
of those who examine those documents.[39]

In another action the same year, NAB urged the FCC to abandon
its proposal that would permit broadcasters to negotiate paid settle-
ments with groups that have filed petitions to deny license renewals.

The NAB's request noted that since citizens' groups were afforded
the legal standing to file petitions to deny license renewals in 1966
(the WLBT-TV case), such groups have

> capitalized upon the use, or threatened use, of
> petitions to deny, to wrest control of programming
> from the stations, dictate employment quotas, force
> the naming of selected individuals to stations' boards
> of directors, obtain free advertising for minority
> businesses and a host of other concessions.[40]

The NAB request noted that the commission's proposal would
have condoned the very activity by which challengers can continue to
pressure licensees into making concessions—consultancy agreements
by which the station pays for the petitioner's advice but simultaneously
runs the risk of giving up essential control of its facility to the challenger. With financial compensation, the NAB said, a "station could
find itself knee deep in consultancies resulting in a prohibitive over-
all price tag and a babble of voices."[41] The NAB requested that the
FCC should take no action on its proposal and said stations still would
remain free to enter into consultancy arrangements if they so desired.

In addition to seeking relief at the congressional level, the
NAB apparently sought protection and support from citizens' group
challenges from other sectors. Officials of NAB have approached
the FCC, segments of the general business community, and members of various publics. All are intertwined, of course, since Congress tends to act when their constituents or vocal special interest
groups desire legislation.

In October 1971, Richard W. Chapin, chairman of NAB's board
of directors, called on the FCC to exercise its responsibilities to
"clearly state that a station need not deal with an organization that
refused to provide documentation (as to membership)." He also asked
the commission to impose penalties on what he termed "extortion
attempts and payoffs." Chapin said the FCC "must back broadcasters
who refuse to accede to demands for control over programming."
Chapin said many broadcasters feel that they must endure meetings
with citizens' groups in which the broadcasters are subject to "name-
calling, obscenities and threats of physical violence" and accused
the FCC of failing to take action to prevent such sessions.[42]

March Evans, chairman of a special NAB task force, and Chapin
also noted that in many license renewal situations the demands of
citizens' groups "come from a central point." They alleged that
"many such demands are written in New York or Washington, and do
not necessarily represent the broadcaster's community. Mr. Evans
referred to a 'coordinated interlocking national movement to displace
current licensees.'"[43] In his task force role, Evans, who is with

Metromedia, Incorporated, planned to attend breakfast meetings in a dozen cities in three weeks in conjunction with a U.S. Chamber of Commerce "aircade" that planned to visit 15 cities for chamber meetings with an anticipated 10,000 businessmen.[44]

Another manner in which some members of the broadcast industry have reacted to citizens' group demands has been in the form of industry cooperation. Broadcasting stated that procedures for license renewals were once a matter between a licensee and his lawyer and now are "virtually an industry-wide convocation. For example, Southern broadcasters, whose licenses are up for renewal next year (1972) are joining together to trade information about methods of ascertainment of local needs, and more important now, how to handle petitions to deny as well as competing applications for existing facilities." Officials from both the NAB and the FCC participated in the South Carolina Broadcasters Association workshop on license renewals.[45]

The Federal Communications Bar Association also appears to be sympathetic to the broadcast industry regarding license renewal challenges. Thomas H. Wall, 1972 bar association president, noted that broadcasting is the "only industry I know where you have to run the gauntlet every three years to stay in business." He said no one has suggested that broadcasters who have not lived up to their responsibilities should be shielded from competition, but he pointed out that those who have made charges against licensees should be compelled to bear the burden of proving them. "If broadcasters give in to the wishes of the protesters too much, they will wind up being led around by the nose." He said the bar group believed Congress should take action to clarify the "confusion and uncertainty" surrounding license renewals.[46] Some members of Congress apparently heeded his message two years later.

HOW SOME STATIONS HAVE REACTED

Although the industry and the NAB generally appear to be hostile to the citizens' movement, they do realize that there could be some justification or merit in some of the specific criticisms and accusations made by various groups. The number of radio and television stations is too large to warrant any absolute conclusions from industry reaction. It probably would be safe, however, to observe that reactions of broadcasters tend to run along several lines. Some broadcasters would steadfastly refuse to accede to the demands of citizens' groups and would be prepared to withstand legally license renewal challenges and FCC proceedings. Others initially might be hostile to citizens' demands; but when actually confronted with the threat of a formal petition to deny license renewal would agree to programming, advertising, or employment policy changes. Other types of broadcasters might cooperate readily with citizens' groups.

As an example of the manner in which some stations have reacted to challenges by citizen coalitions, WHEC-TV and WROC-AM-FM-TV, all in Rochester, New York, in 1972 disputed challenges filed against their license renewals by local citizens' groups. Gannett Company, which owns WHEC-TV, accused Action for a Better Community of using its petition to deny as a "bargaining tool" to procure station financing for a minority youth program that the station already had agreed to broadcast. Rust Craft Broadcasting Company, which owns WROC facilities, argued that a complaint filed by Media Act, a citizens' group, was "defective" in failing to disclose the nature, membership, or purpose of the group. The firm charged that Media Act's brief had statements that "not only reflect misunderstanding, but, perhaps intentional distortion of fact."[47]

One year earlier in California, several Bay area stations maintained that the FCC should not honor the petitions filed against KNBR-AM-FM and KPIX-TV. The television station's spokesman said that the petitioner failed to provide an affidavit in support of his charges. KNBR-AM-FM argued that the station's petitioners—Community Coalition for Media Change, the Bay area chapter of the Japanese-American League, the Oakland Chinese Community Council, and the Mission Media Art—ignored the station's "several invitations to enter into meaningful dialogue."[48]

Another example of an attitude expressed by a broadcast industry executive would be that of Shelton Fisher, president of McGraw-Hill, Incorporated. After McGraw-Hill agreed to changes in employment practices, training, and programming policies concerning racial minority groups, Fisher stated the agreement was the product of a number of meetings held in connection with the company's

> desire to serve fully each of the communities involved. . . . we have reaffirmed and expanded on our plans for programming and employment practices specifically designed to serve all of the people reached by the station. We believe that our operations of these four stations will provide McGraw-Hill with an opportunity to demonstrate its determination to provide outstanding service to the public.[49]

The stations involved are KLZ-TV, Denver, Colorado; WFBM-TV, Indianapolis, Indiana; KOGO-TV, San Diego, California; and

KERO-TV, Bakersfield, California. As noted in Chapter 2, station WOOD-TV, Grand Rapids, Michigan, was dropped from the transaction because of citizens' group protests.

Broadcasting cited the 1972 McGraw-Hill agreement with citizens' groups as probably the "most recent and the most spectacular settlement conducted between a station owner and a citizens' organization . . . that may rival and may exceed any made previously in the history of the citizen movement in broadcasting . . . "[50]

Storer Broadcasting Company, however, suggested that some citizens' groups have attempted to apply "extortion" against broadcast stations. In a pleading with the FCC in response to the commission's proposal that would have sanctioned negotiations between licensees and citizens' groups, whereby the challenger would withdraw its petition to deny in return for a paid "consultancy fee," the Storer legal brief stated that "the kind of consultancy agreement in question here is no more than a money payment extracted as the price for withdrawing a petition to deny—or for not filing one. "[51]

The Storer brief stated, "If citizens' groups have a legitimate role to play in the licensing process—and no broadcaster seriously argues that they do not—it should not be tainted with the prospect of private gain."

In its pleading, the Storer statement noted that in 1970 (one month after the renewal application for one of its stations was filed) the station was approached by a black public relations organization offering to provide counseling with the black community. The public relations representatives asked to be retained at a fee of $1,000 a month for one year. The station declined and one month later the same firm was serving as "spokesman for, and representative of, an 'ad hoc coalition' making 11 demands on all stations in the market." And on another occasion, continued the Storer brief, the broadcast organization was told in attempting to seek interviews with a minority community, "no money, no interviews. "[52]

The Storer statement also noted that its experiences were not unique. According to a trade journal article, Storer said two other cases were similar. In one a Denver, Colorado, Chicano group "offered to withdraw a petition to deny against KWGN-TV there without making any programming or employment demands in return for a direct $15,000 'contribution.' " The other case was in Sandersville, Georgia, where a black group asked the FCC to force WSNT (AM) "to reimburse it for expenses incurred in challenging the station after it had already obtained a non-monetary settlement." Both requests were denied by the commission. [53]

The experiences described by the Storer stations are apparently similar to those of a Portland, Oregon, station KOIN-TV-AM-FM. William Mears, public service director, said a 12 member advisory council representing racial minority groups asked the station to employ a coordinating chairman with a salary of $15,000 to $19,000 a year, plus expenses. Mears said the group also wanted "advisory fees." The station told the group to write up a job description to be considered. KOIN subsequently rejected establishing such a position.[54]

THE EXPERIENCES OF KOIN-TV-AM-FM

At this point it might be helpful to examine the experiences of KOIN-TV-AM-FM whose license was challenged by a citizens' group.

On December 31, 1971, two groups filed a petition with the FCC to deny Mt. Hood Broadcasting Corporation its application for the renewal of its license. The petition was filed on behalf of the United Indian Action Center and New Oregon Publishers. The United Indian Action Center was described as a three-year-old private, nonprofit urban Indian Service Club. New Oregon Publishing Company was formed in 1971 and is the publisher of the monthly Oregon Times.

The petition stated that the station failed to determine the needs, interests, and tastes of the local public. It also accused the station of failing to broadcast enough programs to serve the public interest. It said Mt. Hood Broadcasting Company had aired "insufficient programs" in areas of public affairs generally, locally originated public affairs, and "programming of particular interest to racial and ethnic minorities." The station was also accused of failing to employ "in responsible broadcasting positions" enough members of racial minorities. The challengers said that Portland's two daily newspapers, the Oregon Journal and The Oregonian are "wholly owned by the Newhouse family" and noted that Newhouse owns 50 percent ownership in Mt. Hood Broadcasting, which constitutes effective control of the station. The petition said such ownership was "violative of the anti-monopoly provisions of the Sherman Act."[55] The petition also accused The Oregonian of providing preferential coverage to KOIN's AM radio station. William Mears said the station was not approached or informed before the petition was filed.[56]

Following a series of meetings between station personnel and members of the two groups that signed the petition, the petition was withdrawn in February 1972. The meetings resulted in a formal agreement between the station and groups. The agreement included the establishment of a 12-member advisory council "to advise management on minority matters including problems, needs, and interests and programming and employment by the licensee." The council was composed of four members each from black, Chicano, and Indian groups. The black groups included representatives of the

Portland Black Caucus, the National Association for the Advancement of Colored People (NAACP), The Urban League, and the Black Panther Party. The Indians included the United Indian Action Center, the United Indian Council, the Portland American Indian Club. The Valley Migrant League has four Chicano members, including council Chairman Ester Martinez.[57]

Mears said the station met with the councils four times after March 1972. They met every few months for the first six months, after which time they mutually determined when subsequent meetings would be held. For convenience to the working members, meetings were held in the evening. "During the second meeting, not one member showed up." Mears said he felt the meetings "have not been profitable."[58]

At one of the meetings, Mears said the station offered to air a weekly program to discuss racial minority group problems, but this was rejected by the council. The station next offered to air 30 minutes of prime time each month with the stipulation that the council members handle the production details. That was also rejected by the group. Mears then suggested that the station and council members work together to determine what should be done.[59]

In a statement filed with the FCC, the station pledged,

> KOIN will redouble its efforts affirmatively to seek out new sources of qualified or trainable minority persons to fill vacancies as they occur. In addition to the present sources, such organizations as those belonging to the advisory council, Concentrated Employment Program, and Manpower Training Program will be utilized.

> KOIN policy is to hire the person it considers best suited for the position available, without regard to race, sex, religion, or national origin. However, through the use of additional sources and with the help of the advisory council, KOIN hopes to increase the number of minority employees.

> KOIN has recently completed final transfer of all public affairs activities to one veteran staff member. One of his principal duties will be to develop meaningful public affairs programs and program material for and about the various minorities within the service area.

> KOIN hereby commits itself to an increased emphasis on minority problems, needs and interests during the coming license period. Specifically, it proposes within the next year to increase by at least fifteen percent the broadcast

time devoted to minorities on KOIN-TV over what
was broadcast during calendar year 1971. A good
faith effort will be made to exceed this minimum.

KOIN has recently developed a new local public
affairs program entitled ENCOUNTER, now being
broadcast in prime time. This program, scheduled
twice monthly, deals exclusively with current issues
of interest to the service area. Input from the advisory
council will be utilized to develop ENCOUNTER programs
dealing with minority problems.

KOIN-TV proposes a series of programs dealing with
the history, customs and problems of the various racial
and ethnic groups in Oregon. During each week a program in this series is shown, the KOIN-TV non-entertain-
ment programming will give special attention to the
particular group featured. Again, KOIN will look to its
advisory council for ideas and assistance. These programs
will be broadcast monthly not necessarily consecutively,
until all the significant groups have been covered.

KOIN-TV presently broadcasts in-depth news features on
various local problems, such as Model Cities, welfare,
racial problems, Indian affairs, and ecology. These will
continue and it is anticipated that input from the advisory
council will assist in this area also.

KOIN will work with members of its advisory council, and
others to develop new programs or program series dealing
with the problems, needs and interests of the community.[60]

In dealing with the advisory panel, Mears said he felt the group—
as a group—acted hostilely to him and the station and used obscene
language and insulting mannerisms. Yet in dealing with panel members on an individual basis, he and the president of Mt. Hood Broadcasting Corporation, C. Howard Lane, found them to be personable,
polite, and friendly.

In general, Mears and the station apparently had mixed feelings
in their continuing dialogue with the advisory panel. "Our meetings
have provided us with a different perspective in which we can view
their problems from a new vantage point. We have been sensitized
to their problems and interests," he said.[61] He also questioned how

representative the 12 members actually are of their respective communities. He implied that perhaps members of the NAACP or the Urban League did not really represent the black community in Portland.

On the other hand, he said the station's experiences have forced the station to change its perspective and to reevaluate its employment policies. "We took a look at how many blacks and other minority employees and decided we would hire two more. We ended up employing four, all blacks. We had trouble locating Chicanos and Indians. But our four new employees are making valuable suggestions to us, suggestions that we probably would not have thought of ourselves."[62]

CAPITAL CITIES BROADCASTING

As noted earlier, Capital Cities Broadcasting Corporation, an organization with stations in Philadelphia, New Haven, Connecticut, and Fresno, California, reached an agreement with citizens' groups objecting to the firm's acquisition of stations from Triangle Publications, Inc. The agreement involved a commitment of $1 million over a three-year period to be used in developing programming in cooperation with and for minority groups. It is appropriate to examine in detail the highlights of that agreement.

Joseph P. Dougherty, president of the broadcast division of Capital Cities Broadcasting, stated, "We had had working relationships with minority groups in Buffalo, Houston, and Raleigh-Durham prior to this (one million dollar agreement) and have set similar goals in these markets where we have no written agreement." He described his firm's experiences with citizens' groups as both "rewarding and frustrating."[63]

The agreement stipulated that the money would be used for the "development of programming which reflects the views, aspirations, problems and culture of Black and Spanish-surnamed (Chicano, Puerto Rican, etc.) minority groups within the service area of the three television stations." The stations were WFIL-TV, WNHC-TV, and KFRE-TV.[64] The statement stipulated that the funds to support such programming would be deposited in a minority owned or controlled bank with no less than $333,333 to be deposited each July 1 of the three-year period.

Regarding programming, the agreement said "sufficient program product will be produced to allow each of the subject stations to telecast a minimum of six hours of programming in this field per year (with each program at least one-half hour in length). Capital Cities anticipates and intends that a minimum of 50 percent of such programs will be telecast in prime time. . . . "[65]

Each of the three general managers of the stations were to appoint an advisory committee composed of leaders from the "relevant minority groups within the service area of each station." The committee memberships were to include the broadcast division president of Capital Cities, the general manager of the station, two representatives of the minority organizations in the subject community, and two principal consultants. Then these six persons would agree on a panel of names of minority group leaders to be broadly representative of the minority groups in the communities. The general manager of each station would appoint a group of charter members of the advisory committee from the panel of names drawn up. 66

Station personnel were to meet with the community's advisory committee during the year with "sufficient frequency" to permit discussion of proposals and the presentation of the committee's reactions and criticisms of specific programs "as well as other aspects of station operation which the committee may wish to discuss."

That Capital Cities made a commitment of $1 million to help develop programming for racial minority groups in three communities was to the organization's credit. The firm probably would argue that its interests and concerns for those communities were sincere and genuine. But it also could be argued that Capital Cities may have sought to acquire those three stations regardless of the costs involved in working with racial minority groups. In other words, the long term investment of those stations may have warranted such a commitment. It is impossible to determine the firm's actual motives. Regardless, it is reasonable to conclude that those three communities and the groups involved—as well as the station's personnel—probably were richer as a result of such expenditures and experiences.

Only through experience and time will those communities and stations be able to determine if the agreement and its implementation were satisfactory. To allocate money for the development of programming "which reflects the views, aspirations, problems and culture" of minority groups was a large undertaking, particularly when a minimum of 12 30-minute programs was involved.

Will the leaders from "relevant minority groups" truly represent those groups? Will the station managers meet with the groups with "sufficient frequency" to maintain continuity of interest and membership? Will the stations adequately promote those projected programs to the extent that the groups involved will care to view them? How effective will the programs actually be?

ECONOMIC COSTS INVOLVED

If a station elects to file formally a response to a petition to deny license renewal, it can run into expensive litigation. Station KLZ-TV, Denver, Colorado, was the object of a petition to deny that

station's license renwal. Station officials estimated in 1973 that to
prepare a response to a petition involved about 1,200 man hours.
The station employed college students to review more than 1,000 days
of news scripts and thousands of dollars went for legal fees. The
station manager stated, "With one exception, none of the individual
organizations signing the petition even contacted the station to make
known any of their views, suggestions, and observations . . . which
are so vehemently expressed in the petition."[67]

Charles T. Jones, Jr., vice president of New Mexico Broadcasting Company and general manager of KGGM-AM in Albuquerque,
New Mexico, (the station involved) in 1971 said, "We can't afford
this thing. We literally can't afford it."[68] And Richard Wolfe, president of WBNS AM-FM-TV, Columbus, Ohio, also the object of a
petition, was equally concerned with the cost in time and money involved in confronting community groups. "Everyone, including broadcasters, should be held accountable." He added that since licenses
must be renewed every three years, broadcasters are vulnerable to
that "point of attack" by community groups. And if the attack point
becomes "too vulnerable, the broadcast system as we know it in the
United States will be substantially destroyed or eroded."[69]

To determine the average expenses of stations involved in license
renewal challenges, the NAB surveyed 97 stations that had petitions
to deny filed against them during 1969-71. According to a trade publication, 47 responses were received. An average of 250 man hours
were spent by a single station in opposing a challenge. That figure
ranged as high as 4,000 hours for an individual station. The median
cost in out-of-pocket expenses was $8,300, with individual outlets
reporting a range of $100 to $45,000.[70] Possibly these figures were
inflated or arbitrarily selected. Nevertheless, it would appear that
the cost of challenging petitions can be a major element in a station's
budget.

STATE BROADCAST ASSOCIATIONS

In addition to the NAB, which functions on a nationwide basis,
the broadcasters also have state associations. Perhaps as an indication of how state associations have tended to react to the citizens'
movement, the Oregon Association of Broadcasters (OAB) in 1972
submitted several requests to the FCC regarding citizens' groups
and the radio broadcaster's responsibility to his community.

One of the requests sought the elimination of public files, which
the FCC requires radio stations to maintain locally. The request
noted "public files on each licensee are maintained in Washington,

D.C. In many radio stations there is rarely a request to inspect the
local public file." Also, the OAB requested the elimination of "ascertainment" of local need.

> The present requirement of "ascertainment," etc., is
> not relevant to today's operation of radio. The "ascer-
> tainment" requirement for radio should be eliminated.
> It could be replaced by a narrative statement, properly
> annotated. If the local radio station manager doesn't
> know his local problems and how to meet them, he
> isn't going to be in business very long. Competition
> will automatically take care of the situation.[71]

The state association also sought to change the license period.
"The present three-year license period is too short. A longer period
of five years would lend more stability to the industry. New legislation,
or, FCC rules, are needed to give licensees at least a 'fair shake,'
in license renewal considerations and procedures." The request also
noted that "proposed announcements inviting public criticism of broadcasting would serve no useful purpose."[72]

These three requests need to be examined from a critical viewpoint. The rationale was stated and was, on the surface, self-serving,
designed to facilitate the operation of a station more than to serve
various publics.

First, the request to eliminate the FCC's requirement of stations
maintaining local public files, was based, presumably, on the fact
that such public files are maintained in Washington, D.C., and that
there are few requests to inspect the local files. Both arguments were
without foundation. It would be expensive and time consuming for
citizens of a community to visit Washington, D.C., to inspect documents that could be seen in their communities. Also, that there have
been few requests to inspect local files does not and should not mean
there is no interest, nor that such interest could not occur in the
future. That request apparently was made to discourage local public
inspection.

Second, the OAB's request to eliminate "ascertainment" of local
needs by radio stations also apparently stemmed from selfish interests.
The argument that if a local radio manager did know local problems
he would be out of business and that competition would handle the
situation tends to be fallacious. Competition will not "automatically"
take care of the situation. Broadcasting academician Sydney Head
noted that poorly operated or financially marginal stations can take
a long time to die.[73] And if a station were withering financially, it
would seem doubtful that it could serve the community adequately
while grasping at financial straws.

Finally, the OAB's request that proposed announcements seeking public criticism "would serve no useful purpose" indicated that broadcasters are not very thick-skinned. That statement implies that broadcasters would seek only public approbation; public criticism is to be prevented. This position hardly seems appropriate for a custodian of a public resource licensed to use that resource to serve a local community.

The request to lengthen the license renewal period from three to five years has some merit. If it were approved it could add to more stability in the industry. But conversely, if a station manager refused to serve his community adequately, the viewers or listeners would have to tolerate such performance for a longer period. An argument can be made, which will be noted in Chapter 4, that license periods could be lengthened for stations that are serving their communities in a superior manner.

In summary, OAB's three requests were one-sided and would have had more merit if they had presented all aspects or implications of their merits or lack of merits. They were designed more to deny than to encourage public participation in broadcast matters.

TENTATIVE CONCLUSIONS

If any conclusions are warranted, they would involve the observation that citizens' groups indeed have influenced broadcasting. In an editorial, Broadcasting said "the dissidents won't go away," and added,

> The present system of challenge may be unfair to the incumbent licensee, but it is a rooted fact of life. The broadcaster must cope with it by providing as widely based a program service as he reasonably can afford and his community is likely to accept by resisting demands from groups too small to deserve recognition.[74]

Another conclusion would be that the various publics apparently have benefited from increased communication between citizens' groups and the broadcasters. Citizens' groups have succeeded to the extent of making broadcasters more cognizant of programming for various minority publics and that the mass public is composed of a variety of publics with different interests and needs. As the industry trade journal has observed, "At a minimum, some broadcasters are acknowledging that the pressures brought by the groups have sensitized

them to the need for changes that they might not have otherwise have
made. One station manager whose license is under challenge . . .
stated: 'I am doing my job differently this year than last and will do
it differently next year than this.' The station manager and other
broadcasters across the country express a willingness to provide
programming of interest to minority groups and to hire minority
group members. But in terms of access, they ask, how much is
enough?"[75] A related question he could have asked would be what
type of access to which kinds of decisions.

Mears, of KOIN in Portland, Oregon, stated,

> I'm frankly very pleased with this group (represent-
> atives of black, Chicano, and Indian communities) and
> with what we've discovered so far. We're finding out
> a great deal about minority problems that haven't sur-
> faced before, and about their intensity. They're sen-
> sitizing us to their problems, and that is good.[76]

As noted in Chapter 1, an assumption in this investigation stated
that the manner in which a broadcaster tends to view public participation will vary with how he perceives his role in the area. If he views
his station as being an active community institution, he probably will
be receptive to citizen input. But if he is more concerned with profits,
he probably believes he is doing an adequate job and therefore will not
be too receptive to public participation. The KOIN facility appears
to support this theory since it apparently has improved its services
to the area.

Some stations and broadcasters, such as Mears and Capital
Cities Corporation, have not protested (at least publicly) citizen
involvement. Yet some broadcast trade groups, such as the Oregon
Association of Broadcasters and the NAB, have objected to citizen
participation. Perhaps this has been the result of peer group influences
in which an individual feels obligated to assume formal positions con-
forming to group beliefs and group actions before his colleagues.

Another conclusion that can be drawn is that the NAB has been
changing gradually. One such example is that it has employed its
first black executive. Elbert Sampson, former project director of
the Community Film Workshop in New York, joined NAB in May 1972.
He was previously a special consultant on black issues to the NAB.
Sampson's duties include working with NAB's government relations
and in public relations. The question could be raised whether he
actually has been entrusted with corporate power and decision-making
authority.[77]

Finally, that Congress in 1974 nearly revised the license renewal
period indicates the lobbying power of broadcasters. It also indicates

the seriousness with which NAB and broadcasters view the perceived threat of citizens' groups.

NOTES

1. National Association of Broadcasters, Study Guide on Broadcasting (New York: National Association of Broadcasters, 1966).

2. Letter from Dorothy Lewis, January 27, 1971.

3. Letter from Roy Danish, January 6, 1972.

4. Mal Oettinger, "Inside the FCC," Television/Radio Age, October 30, 1972, p. 78.

5. Ibid.

6. Letter from Robert Kasmire, December 10, 1970.

7. Letter from J. T. Hoover, December 28, 1970.

8. Elton H. Rule, speech delivered to the California Broadcasters Association, Palm Springs, California, January 27, 1972.

9. Ibid.

10. Ibid.

11. Gilbert Seldes, "Public Participation," The Public Opinion Quarterly 24 (fall 1960):9.

12. Letter from Leonard Spinrad, December 16, 1970.

13. Les Brown, Television, The Business Behind the Box (New York: Harcourt, Brace, Jovanovich, 1971), p. 59.

14. Sydney Head, Broadcasting in America (Boston: Houghton Mifflin Co., 1972), p. 352.

15. Richard Jencks, speech delivered to the Broadcasting Industry Symposium, Washington, D.C., January 18, 1971.

16. Ibid.

17. Ibid.

18. Ibid.

19. Nicholas Johnson, How to Talk Back to Your Television Set (New York: Bantam Books, 1970), pp. 200-204.

20. "The Struggle Over Broadcast Access (II)," Broadcasting, September 27, 1971, pp. 24-9.

21. New York Times article printed in the Eugene (Oregon) Register-Guard, October 6, 1971.

22. Roy Danish, speech delivered to the Poor Richard Club, Philadelphia, Pennsylvania, November 11, 1971.

23. Ibid.

24. "ACT Won't Get What It Asked From FCC on Television for Children," Broadcasting, October 7, 1974, p. 15.

25. Letter from Stockton Helffrich, July 6, 1972.

26. Danish speech, op. cit.

27. Ibid.

28. Ibid.

29. "Death of an Industry?", Nation's Business 60, No. 5 (May 1972): 27.

30. Johnson, op. cit., p. 201.

31. "Relief is Just a Senate Bill Away," Broadcasting, October 11, 1971, p. 49.

32. "Hope From the Hill on Renewal Relief," Broadcasting, November 8, 1971, p. 41.

33. "Seven NAB-Type Bills Are Now in The House," Broadcasting, January 31, 1972, p. 30.

34. "Schweiker Renewal Measure Goes Further Than Moss's," Broadcasting, May 8, 1972, p. 36.

35. "Monday Memo," Broadcasting, July 10, 1972, p. 15.

36. "The Dream of Renewal Relief Gets Closer to Reality," Broadcasting, October 14, 1974, p. 19.

37. Ibid.

38. Ibid., p. 20.

39. "NAB Wants FCC to Name Names of File-Checkers," Broadcasting, October 9, 1972, pp. 35-8.

40. "NAB is Thumbs-Down on Payment to Challenger " Broadcasting, October 2, 1972, pp. 35-6.

41. Ibid.

42. "NAB Looks to FCC for Renewal Relief," Broadcasting, October 25, 1971, p. 24.

43. Ibid.

44. Ibid.

45. "Ascertaining Needs of Broadcasters," Broadcasting, November 29, 1971, p. 63.

46. Nation's Business, (May 1972) op. cit., p. 29.

47. "Citizen Shakedown Asserted in Rochester," Broadcasting, June 19, 1972, p. 41.

48. Broadcasting, November 29, 1971, op. cit., p. 61.

49. "McGraw-Hill Sets Record for Concessions to Minorities," Broadcasting, May 15, 1972, p. 26.

50. "The Specialists in Intervention," Broadcasting, May 29, 1972, p. 18.

51. "When Do Challenges Become 'Extortion'?" Broadcasting, October 9, 1972, p. 31.

52. Ibid., p. 32.

53. Ibid.

54. William Mears, public service director, KOIN AM-FM TV, private interview held in Portland, Oregon, October 18, 1972.

55. The Oregonian, January 4, 1972.

56. Mears interview, op. cit.

57. Ibid.

58. Ibid.

59. Ibid.

60. KOIN AM-FM TV, Policy statement filed with the Federal Communications Commission, February, 1972.

61. Mears interview, op. cit.

62. Ibid.

63. Letter from Joseph F. Dougherty, September 29, 1972.

64. Capital Cities Broadcasting Corp., Policy statement filed with the Federal Communications Commission, September, 1972, p. 26.

65. Ibid., p. 29.

66. Ibid., p. 30.

67. Nation's Business, (May 1972) op. cit., p. 28.

68. Broadcasting, September 27, 1971, op. cit., p. 25.

69. Ibid.

70. "Chapin Goes Back Home With Words of Warning," Broadcasting, October 2, 1972, p. 36.

71. Letter from Oregon Association of Broadcasters to Federal Communications Commissioner Richard E. Wiley, July 25, 1972.

72. Ibid.

73. Head, op. cit., pp. 334-5.

74. Broadcasting, September 27, 1971, op. cit., p. 68.

75. Ibid., p. 24.

76. Mears interview, op. cit.

77. "Minorities Get Office at the NAB," Broadcasting, May 1, 1972, p. 41.

CHAPTER

4

REACTIONS OF THE
FCC, THE COMMISSIONERS,
AND THE COURTS TO
CITIZENS'
ORGANIZATIONS

During the period between July 1, 1970, and June 30, 1971, the FCC designated 20 broadcast license renewal applications for hearings—a record number. The commission also denied license renewal for technical violations to eight stations in cases designated for hearing in prior years. Probationary short term renewals were granted to 10 applicants. Field investigations nearly doubled from 27 to 52 in this period. [1]

Prior to the 1969 decision of WLBT-TV, of the cases filed with the FCC complaints by citizens' groups or private parties against stations constituted less than five percent of the total amount; and "most of them were cranks." In 1971, "some 31 out of 80 cases deal either with citizens' complaints or programming matters of the sort that once were considered so far within the FCC's discretion that no reputable lawyer would choose to argue them."[2] As noted in Chapter 1, one FCC commissioner who has served on that agency for a number of years observed that the regulatory atmosphere is "tougher on broadcasting" than it has ever been in his nearly two decades of service. [3]

Indeed, in September 1974, for the first time in its history, the FCC unofficially decided not to renew a broadcast license on the basis of complaints from a citizens' organization. The decision involved a public television licensee—held by the Alabama Educational Television Commission (AETC). In a four-to-two vote, eight licenses and one construction permit held by the state commission were denied renewal.

The issues involved in the denial centered on (1) whether the state commission engaged in a pattern of racial discrimination in employment practices, (2) whether the AETC served community needs, and (3) whether the FCC should consider during its deliberations evidence designed to prove that the state body had improved substantially its services after complaints were filed in 1970. [4]

The FCC vote reversed an initial ruling of an FCC administrative law judge, who found in 1973 that there was not a deliberate discriminatory policy by AETC but that it had failed to meet the needs of blacks. He recommended that the license be renewed because AETC had upgraded its service after the complaint. [5]

Broadcasting reported that the FCC's decision created two "virtually unprecedented elements." The first was that the FCC had never before removed a license of a noncommercial station; the second was that the FCC "would be giving citizens' groups a go-ahead of sorts to step up their activities against broadcast licensees."[6] The FCC denied the renewal of the WLBT (TV) license in 1969 only after the United States Court of Appeals directed the commission. The question could be asked why the FCC decided to apply the ultimate sanction against a noncommercial station rather than a commercial station, although the commission has denied licenses of commercial stations and applicants for technical reasons and not on the basis of citizens' groups complaints. However, this study does not involve noncommercial broadcasting.

It seems reasonable to assume that the field of commercial, and more recently non-commercial broadcasting and the regulation of that industry has been in the process of change. How has the FCC tended to respond to citizens' groups? What policies has it adopted or failed to adopt? What role have the courts played regarding public participation?

Before examining those areas, it might be helpful to return to a point introduced in Chapter 1, which attempted to explain the relationship between the public, the broadcaster, and the FCC. The FCC, it was noted, has been criticized for failing to oversee consistently the use of the airwaves and for tending to issue decisions more favorable to broadcasters than to the public. Les Brown noted,

> The American broadcaster is one part conscience and
> nine parts profit-motive. . . . In his defense is the
> fact that the broadcaster did not begin with the in-
> tention of plundering the airwaves. He was simply
> allowed to indulge in bad habits by an inattentive
> government; a historically apathetic sometimes
> even sympathetic, regulatory agency, the Federal
> Communications Commission; and an abstruse
> Communications Law dating to 1934, written
> before anyone could foresee television . . . [7]

Economist Ronald H. Coase observed that a regulatory commission cannot be expected to act in the public interest since "it must inevitably adopt certain policies and organizational forms which condition its thinking and limit the range of its policies. . . . It is difficult to operate closely with an industry without coming to look at its problems in industry terms." He added that the FCC is uncomfortably aware that "all is not well. And so it has exhorted the businessmen to act in the public interest, and incidentally, against their own."8

Brown's description of the Communications Act as "abstruse" was an apt observation. One of the provisions of the act limited the FCC to grant broadcast licenses renewals for a period of not less than three years. The act was amended by Congress in 1960, which gave the commission authority to issue licenses for shorter periods. Marcus Cohn, Washington attorney specializing in broadcast matters, noted that this amendment—and the act—means that the commission is still unable to grant license renewals for longer periods, a possible means of rewarding stations providing "superior" service to a community.

Cohn argued that the "entire thrust of the Communications Act and of the FCC regulatory policies has accentuated the negative. All passing students get the same grade, although the poorer students receive various kinds of black marks. But no one gets an A for succeeding, much less for trying hard." He added that the end result of this policy has been to "dampen enthusiasm for excellence. The Commission should have some carrots to pass out to outstanding broadcasters."9

Cohn's observations appear to have some merit. Combined with Coase's statements, it could be observed that whatever shortcomings the FCC has evidenced, not all blame should fall on the commission or the commissioners. Perhaps the system, the structure, and the Communications Act need to be examined.

EARLY FCC REACTIONS

Against this background, it would be appropriate to explore how the FCC, the courts, and other government offices have reacted to citizens' councils. Historically, the commission tended to encourage citizens' groups. As noted in Chapter 2, the commission recommended,

> Radio listener councils can also do much to improve the
> quality of program service. Such councils, notably in
> Cleveland, Ohio, and Madison, Wisconsin, have already
> shown the possibilities of independent listener organiza-
> tions. First, they can provide a much needed channel
> through which listeners can convey to broadcasters the

wishes of the vast but not generally articulate radio
audience. Second, listener councils can engage in
much needed research concerning public tastes and
attitudes. Third, listener councils can check on the
failure of network affiliates to carry outstanding network sustaining programs and on the local programs
substituted for outstanding network sustaining programs. . . . Fourth, they can serve to publicize
and to promote outstanding programs—especially
sustaining programs which at present suffer a
serious handicap for lack of the vast promotional
enterprise which goes to publicize many commercial
programs. Other useful functions would also no doubt
result from an increase in the number and an extension
of the range of activities of listener councils, cooperating with the broadcasting industry but speaking solely
for the interest of listeners themselves. [10]

Four years later—in 1950—FCC Chairman Wayne Coy regretted
the scarcity of listener and viewing councils. "The sad truth of the
matter is that this business of listener participation in improving
our broadcasting service is largely an unexplored field." Speaking
to a meeting of the Institute for Education by Radio at Ohio State
University, Coy stated,

You have here some admirable pioneers in the world.
You are a courageous band but your number is far too
few. I would like to see this particular session of the
Institute for Education by Radio go down in radio history
as the springboard for an aggressive, all-out nationwide campaign to establish listener councils in every
city in America. [11]

Coy said a national system of councils would wield a

powerful influence for good. . . . This would be
a dramatic demonstration of the function of the
democratic process. It would be a shining example
of free citizens of a free nation exercising their
freedom to look and listen. Such organizations
could be of great assistance not only to the industry
and to the Federal Communications Commission, but
to the Congress which writes our radio laws. I would
like to see these listener groups represented at hearings
in their communities involving applications for new

stations, or for renewal of license of present stations,
or for transfer of control of existing stations. I would
like to see them well represented in hearings before
the Commission in Washington and in every discussion
involving changes in our broadcasting polcies.[12]

The FCC chairman also issued several precautions concerning
potential council members. He suggested that potential members

must study the radio laws and rules so that you will
know what a licensee's responsibility is and what the
public's rights are. You must acquire an understanding
of the practical business of broadcasting. . . . You
must seek the advice of the specialists in the various
fields in your community so that your judgment will
be based upon facts and expert opinion. . . . while
listener councils should cooperate on a friendly basis
with local broadcasters in the interest of community
betterment, it must maintain complete independence.
It must keep free of all entangling alliances.[13]

Given the encouragement and enthusiasm with which FCC Chairman Coy described the council movement, it could be asked, "why
didn't the number or the thrust of the councils increase?" There is
no easy answer although one possible explanation might be that the
"Blue Book" failed to carry much impact in the broadcast industry.
Indeed, Charles Siepmann, who helped author the book, observed
that the FCC has failed to implement the guidelines in the book.[14]
Another possible explanation might be that the commission, in
its subsequent actions, failed to encourage the development of the
council movement by not holding license renewal hearings in local
communities and inviting public participation. At one time, however,
the FCC did attempt briefly to hold local hearings and invited third
parties to participate but the policies were discontinued.
Former FCC Commissioner Clifford Durr noted that after
World War II, the FCC

started an experiment to see whether we could get more
of an expression from the community where the station
was to be located. A number of members of the Commission sat as hearing officers just for their own education. It was quite enlightening. The response was
very good. The local newspapers would carry the story
that the FCC was going to have a hearing and that people
were invited to come.

It was dropped because of "the pressure of business in Washington, because of the flood of application grants that came in after the war. . . . We were swamped."[15]

To indicate the shift in the apparent attitude of the FCC from previous enthusiasm to one of indifference regarding citizens' groups in the 1950s, Rosel Hyde, who was then on the commission stated, "I would say an organized group would not have any standing to go to court. . . . You must remember that the basic principle of the Communications Act is to place the interest of the community as a whole above that of any individual or group."[16]

Hyde's views were supported by Benedict P. Cottone, former general counsel of the FCC,

> The court's position on these matters (regarding the public interest) is that Congress has laid down a responsibility for the agency to administer. The courts are not going to interfere with that agency's judgment as to what is the "public interest, convenience or necessity" unless you have such an outrageous and unreasonable interpretation that it becomes necessary. . . . an Agency can be reversed only if it commits error of law. On the face of it, there must be a complete violation of some statutory requirement or a complete denial of a fair hearing, before the courts will act. . . . A listener does not have a standing to appeal.[17]

The statements of Hyde and Cottone appear to reflect the general attitude of the FCC after the "Blue Book" was issued as it entered a less active phase. Possibly because of the controversy that resulted when that publication was issued, the commission seemed to be preoccupied with the 1948-52 freeze in television or in other matters. Meyer Weinberg stated, "American industry in mid-1946 was in no mood to take on additional regulation that would moderate its dedication to commercialism. The broadcasting industry thus found support in the increasingly conservative cast of national politics. As a consequence, the FCC spoke no more about the Blue Book. . . . in the years after 1946, the FCC didn't even choose to issue protests."[18]

As noted in Chapter 1, American society began to show an interest in consumerism in the 1960s, and this interest gradually was applied to the commercial broadcast industry. Possibly detecting or reflecting this interest, the FCC renewed its interest in how broadcasters were serving "the public interest, convenience and necessity." And in areas where the FCC failed to act, or acted in an accountable manner, appeals were filed by citizens' groups with the courts. Court decisions have reversed FCC policies, forcing the commission to adopt new policies or regulations. These and major decisions of the FCC adopted during the 1960-70 decade will next be examined. The role of the courts and how individual commissioners perceive citizens' councils will then be explored.

RECENT FCC DECISIONS

In 1960—one year after the FCC held hearings on the quiz show scandals that brought public attention to the industry—the commission announced its 1960 Programming Policy Statement, which placed more emphasis on the broadcasters' duty to ascertain and fulfill community needs and interests. The statement stressed the importance of broadcasters determining the "tastes, needs and desires of the public in his community and to provide programming to meet those needs and interests."[19]

In 1961, FCC Chairman Newton Minow succeeded in calling public attention to the problems of broadcasting in his "vast wasteland" speech delivered at an NAB meeting.[20] By calling attention to the industry, Minow seemingly succeeded in stepping up increased regulatory activity by the commission. Such activities include the application of the fairness doctrine to cigarette commercials, which led to the ultimate ban of all such commercials; an inquiry into ownership of broadcast facilities by conglomerates having extensive outside business interests; the adoption of rules for the first time prohibiting ownership of stations in different services (AM, FM, TV) in the same community; a notice of proposed rule-making that would require divestiture of broadcast or newspaper holdings, so a single party may own only a newspaper, a TV, or a radio station in the same city or area; and other decisions.[21] Many of these decisions were reached in 1969, apparently a pivotal year for the FCC.

SOME FCC REJECTIONS

Concerning the specific area of citizens' groups and their rights to participate in license renewal matters, the FCC was forced to reverse its 1964 policy of denying legal standing to such groups by the United States Court of Appeals in 1969. Since that decision, the commission has granted standing to citizens' bodies, but the complaints and petitions of citizens' groups have not always been successful at the FCC. In several cases the commission has rejected petitions.

For example, in October 1971, the FCC denied a request by Alianza Federal de Puebles Libres to open the financial records of three Albuquerque, New Mexico, television stations whose license renewals the group was considering challenging. [22] And in another instance, the commission rejected the protests by citizens' groups and renewed the licenses of WWJ-TV, Detroit, and WTCJ-TV, Atlanta, Georgia. Broadcasting said the complaints in those two cases were similar to each other and to many that are holding up license renewals of more than 100 stations. Both stations were accused of neglecting to ascertain the community needs, especially those of the black community, and of discriminatory employment practices. [23]

An in another case, the FCC told two California citizens' groups that they were unable to file a petition to deny the license renewal application of KERO-TV, Bakersfield, after the November 1, 1971 deadline. The groups failed to meet the deadline. [24]

OTHER FCC ACTIONS

The commission, in addition to accepting or rejecting the petitions of citizens' groups, has taken some actions that possibly are designed to facilitate and expedite both commission action and citizens' groups approaching the FCC.

The FCC, in one example, studied the feasibility of establishing an office to counsel members of the public on any matters over which the FCC has jurisdiction. The office would serve individuals who have complaints about broadcasting by informing them of their rights and advising them on how to seek satisfaction or redress. Briefly described earlier, a six-man committee was appointed by former FCC Chairman Burch to suggest means for streamlining commission procedures. Conceivably, the office could advise complainants on procedures to follow in filing petitions to deny license renewals. But it would not serve as an advocate to represent the complainant in proceedings before the commission. [25]

The FCC also established in 1971 a task force on children's programming headed by Elizabeth Roberts. The task force would assist in developing and recommending policy recommendations to the FCC. [26]

Also noted earlier was the FCC's decision to issue a public notice of proposed rule making as a result of an Action for Children's Television (ACT) request. It was issued on February 12, 1970. But in October, 1974, the commission rejected requests that it establish regulations aimed at improving children's television programs. Instead, it proposed publishing a general guideline asking broadcasters to devote a "reasonable amount" of programming for children.

The FCC's proposed guideline, which is still subject to change, also approves the NAB's advertising code for children's programs. The code, adopted by the NAB, would reduce advertising for children's Saturday and Sunday programs from 12 to nine and one-half minutes an hour beginning January 1976. On weekday afternoons, the advertising would drop from 16 to 12 minutes an hour in 1976. [27]

The president of ACT, Peggy Charren, said the FCC's decision is "better than nothing, but hard rules are needed." And two broadcast industry lawyers (who asked not to be identified) said the FCC guideline would provide local consumer groups a valuable new wedge to use in challenging license renewals of stations that fail to broadcast adequate programming for children. [28]

The recent FCC document reportedly includes a study by a commission economist that states that the networks did not lose money when they previously reduced advertisements on children's television programs from 16 to 12 minutes an hour. The study is said to assert that the networks made up for the actual loss in advertising time by increasing advertising charges. [29]

In January 1970, the commission issued another significant policy statement that would apply in comparative hearings between applicants for renewal of a station's license and competing new applicants for the same facilities. The policy specified that where the renewal applicant could show a service substantially attuned to the needs of the community area, and without serious deficiencies in other respects, the station would be preferred at renewal time. But in June 1971, the United States Court of Appeals overturned that policy. According to the court, the policy violated the Communications Act by denying a hearing to qualified applicants. [30]

Former Commissioner Johnson opposed the policy, and before it was reversed by the court said the effect of the policy statement "is to discourage citizen participation in the license renewal process." [31]

In March 1971, the commission issued a revised "Primer on Ascertainment of Community Problems by Broadcast Applicants." The primer described in detail how broadcasters may or may not determine local issues and needs to use as guidelines in local programming. [32]

After a two-year study, the FCC in May 1973 adopted a new set of rules designed to give more meaning to the broadcast license renewal process. The new regulations require radio and television stations to make continuing announcements about their obligations to the public and about the public's right to complain to the station and to the commission. Broadcasters are now required to file for renewal four months in advance of license expiration of the old license, rather than the previously required three months. The FCC said the purpose of such a change is to provide community groups "ample time" to examine renewal applications, "discuss any problems with the licensees and, if desired, to file timely applications to deny" the renewal. The FCC also eliminated the rule requiring stations to publish notice of the license applications in a newspaper. All such announcements will be broadcast every 15 days throughout their license period describing their public service obligations and inviting comments and suggestions.

Commenting on the need for the announcements on a continuing basis, the FCC noted that since the new rules were issued, the number of petitions to deny broadcast renewal applications had continued to increase. "The most common complaints were that licensees had not met the needs of significant segments of their service areas. By requiring the announcements, the Commission is attempting to insure that licensees will 'remain conversant' with community problems and that citizens will be encouraged to communicate their problems to licensees and attempt to resolve local problems as they arise."[33]

Both television and radio licensees are required to ascertain community needs in accordance with the FCC's 1971 primer. Stations, however, will not be required to file such ascertainment reports with the commission, but they will certify to the FCC that they have followed the commission's guidelines in station surveys. The information will be made available to the public.[34]

Moreover, under the annual reporting requirements for commercial television stations, licensees will have to place each year, in their public inspection file, a list of significant programs and the needs of their service areas and the stations' typical and illustrative programs presented to meet those needs. Stations will also be required to compile a statistical breakdown of the types of programs presented in various categories. The FCC hopes by this means "to develop a mechanism by which the licensee's conception of current significant community programs and needs and his efforts to meet them could be made available to the public on a continuing basis."[35]

Regarding the banning of commercials from children's programs, an FCC staff report issued in July 1972, stated the television networks would lose about $75 million annually in advertising revenue if commercials were "totally banned from those programs—a loss which could cause them to drop kid's shows entirely."[36] The report appeared to undermine a request by ACT.

The FCC's report was made at the request of Chairman Burch in response to ACT's petition. The report stated that the only way networks would regain their money if commercials for children were eliminated would be to increase advertising prices in prime time and daytime television, or to drop children's programming completely. The networks apparently did just that—increased advertising fees.

Charren, ACT's president, in reply to the FCC report said, "It deals only with today's problems of financing but doesn't speak to tomorrow's possibilities. . . . Why should networks profit from children's TV? The rotten programming that is on now costs money? What ACT wants to do is make a fundamental change in the system by which children's TV is financed."[37]

That the FCC issued a notice of proposed rule making and that it did make a study of ACT's proposals was in itself significant. Although it was possible that ACT's request to ban commercials from children's programs would not be met, that the NAB Code Review Board and the FCC have taken notice of ACT's proposal could be indicative that changes could take place.

Saturday Review columnist Robert Lewis Shayon observed that if the FCC were to interject itself in decisions of the type or caliber of children's programs it could create a questionable precedent. Such action could be interpreted as opening the door for the commission to rule on other types of programming. "In justifying its failure to act (historically), the FCC has traditionally cited the Communications Act of 1934, which bars the Commission from censorship and excludes stations from common carrier law."[38] He noted if the FCC did take action regarding children's programming it must state that children are a special audience and such action would not be considered a precedent.

Perhaps as a result of some of the petitions and complaints from citizens' groups involving minority publics, the FCC in July 1972 wrote to 30 stations in Pennsylvania and Delaware for more information concerning the stations' efforts to provide equal employment opportunity to women and members of minority groups.[39] The stations, which include three television stations, had reported no minority group or women employees in reports submitted for 1971 and 1972.

The FCC, in a public notice announcing the equal employment opportunity inquiry, said the notice had two objectives: the first was to evaluate the effectiveness of the stations' employment programs; the second was to help the commission obtain an insight into problems stations were encountering in locating minority employees. The notice stated, "Based on the experience gained, the Commission will be in a position to determine whether further action is necessary to effectuate equal employment opportunity for minority persons and women."[40]

The FCC new "Primer on Ascertainment of Community Problems by Broadcast Applicants" incorporated ideas that had been advocated by former commissioners Robert Bartley and Kenneth Cox. Television/Radio Age said the area of ascertainment had been a "hazy one, usually handled on a case-by-case basis." The trade journal noted that the primer had been requested by private lawyers to help

their broadcast clients—or complainants. The commissioners themselves issued qualifying statements of endorsement, and not all indicated they would fully support it. The magazine said the "Commission is receptive to floating a trial balloon in this area," although they
may not approve of the final product. The primer provided that television stations (it did not include radio) would be required to devote a
certain percentage of broadcasting to news and public affairs under
a proposed formula.[41]

Regarding the primer's proposal that the broadcaster would
be required to air announcements explaining how the public may
express its opinions on broadcast service, one broadcaster said this
would be "placing our own head on the block!" according to the
magazine. The commission calls it an effort to "ensure continuing
dialogue . . . between the licensee and the community."[42]

Also the primer stated the FCC would consider community feedback at television license renewal times, which the licensee has
solicited. The commission would compare promises with performance
and inspect percentages of programming in the "critical programming
categories" local programs, news, public affairs, and so on. The
commission would "closely scrutinize the renewal applicants whose
rankings fall below an appropriate level (e.g. 10 percent)."

Possibly to encourage the proposal, the FCC in September
1972 issued a procedural manual, "The Public and Broadcasting," an
eight-page booklet which defines the responsibilities of the licensee,
the commission, and the public. The publication was issued to help
the public and discussed in detail the procedures involved if a person
or group wishes to participate in license renewal proceedings. It
stated,

> In the manual, an effort is made to outline the respective
> roles of the broadcast station, the Commission, and the
> concerned citizen in the establishment and preservation
> of quality broadcasting services, to outline procedures
> available to the citizen, and to provide practical advice
> concerning their use. We are hopeful that the manual
> will encourage participation by members of the com-
> munity and that it will direct such participation along
> lines which are most effective and helpful to the com-
> mission.[43]

Commissioner Richard E. Wiley (1974 Chairman) said the
manual "reiterates the theme of the 'Blue Book' proposals that
discussion at the local level offers the greatest promise for broadcasting in the public interest, and while not intended as a substitute
for the Commission's Rules of Practice and Procedure, it represents

the current procedures and policies of the Commission with respect to broadcast licensee responsibility."[44]

That the FCC issued a how-to-do-it manual encouraging citizen participation indicated the commission indeed was interested in having members of the public voice concerns of broadcasting and in having them become involved in how stations perform. The FCC's work-load regarding license renewal proceedings has increased significantly within the past several years. Possibly to alleviate its burden, the commission in the fall of 1972 suggested that if licensees and their challengers settled their differences in their communities, "the backlog in processing renewal applications would diminish."[45] The proposal would allow broadcast licensees and parties contesting the license re-newal applications to negotiate their grievances on a private basis, without FCC action, and would permit stations to compensate chal-lengers if the petitioners withdraw their challenges.

According to Broadcasting, many broadcasters disagreed with the proposal and advanced two arguments. "First, it was contended, the potential for abuse of the proposed compensation policy on the part of the citizen groups outweighs the possible benefits. Second, if the Commission implements the proposal it would be abdicating to outside parties its responsibility to oversee the operation of its li-censees."[46]

The Office of Communications of the United Church of Christ, however, strongly favored the Commission's proposal. It pointed out that it has always encouraged the parties it aids to negotiate privately with broadcasters and noted that an "overwhelming majority" of peti-tions to deny filed with the FCC are subsequently withdrawn following private agreements.[47]

THE FAIRNESS DOCTRINE

Perhaps the most difficult and most controversial area the FCC has had to deal with during the last decade has been its own fairness doctrine. This doctrine has been subject of much dispute by many groups involved with broadcasting—advertisers, political parties, courts, citizens' groups, the commission, and the Federal Trade Commission. There are cases pending before the United States Supreme Court involving a legal interpretation of the doctrine and its applicability to broadcasting. Before discussing specific cases, a brief review of the doctrine might be helpful. According to the commission,

the Fairness Doctrine has evolved over some 40 years
as the guiding principle in assuring to the public an opportunity to hear contrasting views on controversial
issues of public importance. Enunciated as early as
1929 by the Federal Radio Commission, the doctrine
was most fully fleshed out in The Report on Editorial-
izing by Broadcast Licensees, 13 FCC 1246 (1949) and
has been sustained by the U.S. Supreme Court in the
Red Lion Broadcasting Co. Case.

The Fairness Doctrine is grounded in the recognition
that the airwaves are inherently not available to all who
would use them. It requires that those given the privilege
to access hold their licenses and use their facilities as
trustees for the public at large, with a duty to present
discussion of public issues and to do so fairly by afford-
ing reasonable opportunity for the presentation of conflict-
ing views by appropriate spokesmen. . . . The guiding
premise as the Supreme Court put it, is not "unabridg-
able First Amendment right to broadcast comparable to
the right of every individual to speak, write or publish,
but rather the right of the public to receive suitable access to social, political, esthetic, moral and other ideas
and experiences. . . . "48

This was the view of the United States Supreme Court in the
Red Lion Case in 1969. In that landmark case, the court enunciated
two bases for the fairness doctrine: first, that broadcast facilities
must operate in the public interest; second, that under the First
Amendment, the public has a right to free and open debate. That
decision affirmed the FCC's ruling of the Cullman rule, which
stipulated that suitable opposing views must be put on the air at the
licensee's own expense if sponsorship is unavailable.[49] The commission stated that to invoke the fairness doctrine all parties must
recognize that there exists a "controversial issue of public notice"
on which the licensee has refused to allow the presentation of a
reasonably balanced point of view.

Various groups within the last several years have attempted to
apply the doctrine in purchasing or acquiring airtime to run counter
commercials opposing the war in Vietnam, to counter automobile
gasoline commercials, and other causes. In one decision, the FCC
denied the request of the Business Executives Move for Peace (BEM)
to purchase time to counter the president's views on the U.S. role
in Vietnam. The commission said licensees need not sell time to
individuals and parties, but the United States Court of Appeals

reversed that decision.[50] In May 1973, the United States Supreme
Court, in a seven-to-two decision, ruled that broadcasters are not
required to accept paid advertisements on public issues such as war
or politics.

In reversing the United States Court of Appeals decision, the
nation's highest court stated that giving everyone access to broadcast advertising facilities might lead to monopolization of the airways
by those best able to afford it. Chief Justice Warren Burger also
noted that unlimited access could inject more government control
over the broadcast media, since access involves the freedom of speech
issue. The decision was applauded by broadcasters who viewed it
as a "serious if not fatal blow to the movement on the part of some
citizen groups and public-interest group lawyers seeking to establish
a right of access to the broadcast media . . . "[51]

Tracy Westen, of the Stern Community Law Firm that represented BEM, saw the court ruling differently: "This decision will allow
the broadcaster to focus on making money with less to worry about
in terms of community service." He also noted that the decision
left citizens' groups two remaining avenues in which to seek "diversity"
in commercial programming. One is for citizens' groups to file
petitions to deny license renewal; the other is to attack cross-channel
affiliation or multiple owners on concentration of control.[52]

An FCC attorney agreed with Westen that the Supreme Court's
ruling could result in an escalation of petitions to deny licenses but
suggested that since nonrenewal is so severe the commission
could be more reluctant to deny licenses. Both Westen and the FCC
lawyer agreed that commercial broadcasters should not regard the
BEM decision as carte blanche to ignore controversial public issues
or to discriminate against racial minorities.[53]

Prior to the Supreme Court's BEM decision, Burch stated,
"Bluntly, we face a chaotic mess," referring to the fairness doctrine.

Another problem area of citizens' group activity that illustrates
both the concern of the FCC and the courts has been the question of
whether citizens' groups challenging broadcast license renewals
should be reimbursed by the stations.

In 1970, the commission denied approval of an agreement in
which KTAL-TV, Texarkana, Texas, would have paid the United
Church of Christ $15,000 as reimbursement for aid to a number of
citizens' black groups that had petitioned to deny the station's renewal application. The commission stated there is "no statutory
guide" for approving the reimbursement request. But the United
States Court of Appeals subsequently reversed the FCC's decision
and sent the matter back to the commission.

Chief Judge David L. Bazelon, writing for the three-judge
panel, told the FCC that it cannot lay down a "principle of general
application" that such reimbursements were not in the public interest.

The ruling directed the FCC to determine whether this specific case might warrant some type of reimbursement. The case was remanded to the commission for the specific purpose of determining whether the church's submitted expenses were "legitimate and prudent."[54]

In May 1972, the FCC issued a combined notice of inquiry and notice of proposed rule making asking for suggestions on whether reimbursement, if allowed, should be limited to a responsible organization filing a meritorious, good-faith petition to deny. The commission also asked for comments on whether it should limit the dollar amount to be reimbursed, whether the agreements should be reviewed periodically, whether the agreement should specify the services a group is expected to perform, and whether it should be limited in time.

According to Broadcasting, the FCC's concern about possible abuses resulting from financial agreements was reflected in the statement that service to the public was a "critical consideration," one that could "conceivably be skewered by a party's interest in future sums to be garnered" under an agreement. The commission added that such agreements could contribute to the licensees' sensitivity to local needs.[55]

Although private agreements reached between citizens' groups and broadcast stations might appear to have many merits in theory, there are at least two troublesome aspects to the concept. Broadcasters might be tempted to "buy off" with bribes or some other type of reward for the group or its spokesman. And the spokesman of the citizens' group might be equally tempted to accept such an offering.

Also, compensation to a citizens' group would be yet another factor or consideration involved in a complicated situation between public participation and broadcasting. Broadcasters naturally would feel inclined to be against legal compensation and claim they could not afford an added expense. Yet citizens' groups, lacking their own legal expertise or monies to employ legal counsel, feel such compensation would be warranted since they are seeking proper allocation of a public resource. There appears to be no simple solution to this aspect of the problem.

SUMMARY OF FCC ACTIONS

As the foregoing has attempted to indicate, the FCC apparently has attempted to be impartial in dealing with citizens' groups. Both former FCC Chairman Burch and ex-Commissioner Johnson, two outspoken members, have suggested that broadcasting and the regulation of that industry would be improved through more public participation. Referring to the fairness doctrine, columnist Shayon noted that the FCC's position "was not an easy one. A majority of the commissioners seemed responsive to the TV industry, which argued that to grant access to the public would drastically alter the broadcasting system. Yet the cultural climate in which the Communications Act was originally written forty years ago has itself been altered radically." He notes that the Act applied to a different culture and that we now have different sets of values.

> The myth of the two cultures in broadcasting dies hard, but it is dying. More and more citizens realize that this nation's goals are set not only by the programs explicitly devoted to public issues but . . . by the "virtual free-fire-zone" of advertising and even by the "cloying blandness" of general programming.[56]

Shayon's observation that the Communications Act may be out of date tends to coincide with that of Clay Whitehead, formerly of the President's Office of Telecommunications Policy. The NAB and members of Congress also have sought to change or amend the Act, for possibly different reasons. But all apparently have felt some change in the Communications Act of 1934 is needed.

Communications attorney Cohn noted that many groups of concerned citizens have complained to the commission about the performance of stations; and these complaints have had an impact on commission decisions. "Several stations have either been denied the renewal of their licenses or have been given licenses for less than three years because of adverse comments from the public." Cohn, as mentioned earlier, suggested that if the FCC were empowered to renew station licenses for more than three years, the public "would have an opportunity to promote the recognition of outstanding stations."[57] This would also entail changing or amending the Communications Act.

Former FCC Commissioner Robert T. Barley, who served on the commission 20 years and retired June 30, 1972, helped author the revised proposed primer on how broadcasters would ascertain community needs. He noted prior to his retirement that the "old timers (in broadcasting) knew what was going on in their communities and served the needs." The new broadcasters lack such awareness, and this has helped contribute to the citizens' group movement. Another factor he mentioned was that the contemporary broadcaster tends to be more interested in business than in broadcast service. "If broadcasters had had a Bartley primer and paid attention to it 15 years ago, there wouldn't have been a WLBT case."[58]

The Harvard Journal on Legislation has pointed out that some of the difficulties faced by citizens' groups tend to stem more from operational realities of the FCC than from other problems.

> The decisions of the FCC may be subject to the vagaries of shifting ideological composition and the impact of change in national administrations. Moreover, pervasive broadcasting industry influence stifles impartiality.[59]

The Journal also noted that another disadvantage of the administrative-judicial process has been the commission's employment of warnings rather than more stringent sanctions against offending licensees, although warnings alone can sometimes be effective.

> Politics and industry lobbying probably account for the infrequent use of the intermediate remedies (such as short-term licenses, cease-and-desist orders and fines) which Congress entrusted to the FCC. But the very nature of licensing is probably the primary reason for failure to invoke more severe sanctions. . . . As a remedy it (suspension or license revocation) has been traditionally reserved for only the most extreme cases.

> The FCC has effectively relinquished to local citizens the primary guardianship of the public interest in community orientation of broadcasting at least in part because of its lack of resources to conduct this type of investigatory surveillance. A local group, in contrast, is well equipped for the task: it has available television and radio receivers, volunteer viewers and listeners and the necessary time.[60]

In a letter to station KTAL-TV, Texarkana, a station that agreed to a number of programming and policy changes after a citizens' group agreed to withdraw its petition, the FCC wrote in 1969,

> We believe that this Commission should encourage licensees to meet with community oriented groups to settle complaints of local broadcast service. Such cooperation at the community level should prove to be more effective in improving local service than would be the imposition of strict guidelines by the Commission. In view of the resolution of the matters filed against KTAL-TV and the measures adopted to improve the television service to Texarkana, the Commission has granted your application for renewal. . . .

You are cautioned, however, that your performance
during this period will be carefully examined at the
end of the license term to determine whether you
have made an affirmative and diligent effort to serve
the needs and interests of the city to which KTAL-TV
is licensed. [61]

Commissioner Johnson, in a separate concurring statement said,

I support the majority's disposition of this case because
it represents a first effort at a commendable innovation
in the process of public participation in the license renewal process. Hearings are cumbersome, expensive,
and truly a last resort—for licensee and contestant
alike. [62]

This appears to have been the pattern of the commission. It
appeared to encourage public participation, but yet it was reluctant
to assume policy positions that could interject the FCC into a dispute
between a licensee and a complainant. The commission, did, however, issue a proposed revised primer on how broadcasters ascertain
community needs. It has not been adopted; and even if it should adopt
the primer, it would be effective only to the extent that such rules
were enforced.

In summary, the FCC's activities indicate that the commission
has assumed a more active stance regarding how broadcasters serve
their local communities. Perhaps the key concept that can be detected
in the major decisions would be "access." The commission used the
term in several decisions.

That the FCC has been more interested in having the use of the
airwaves better serve the public during the 1960-70 decade has appeared certain. In a larger context, it is safe to observe that the FCC,
as other governmental agencies, public institutions, and some private
industries, has been forced into a more active posture through a
better informed and educated society. Contemporary society places
more emphasis on the public as consumers and on a more judicious
and equitable use of public resources—including the airwaves.

Broadcasting academician Head wrote that "consumerism is
here to stay, and many of the administrative-agency reforms . . .
can be expected to go into effect. This will mean increased public
participation in licensing and other key FCC decisions. Similarly,
more public participation in program decisions is likely to follow. . . . "[63]

It is clearly not without significance that the FCC voted to deny
the license renewal of the Alabama Educational Television Commission—particularly on the basis of citizens' group complaints. It is

also not without significance that the FCC selected a noncommercial station to apply the ultimate weapon against a broadcaster. Conceivably, the commission could be flexing its muscles.

THE COMMISSIONERS' VIEWS

Regarding the views of the individual seven commissioners, each should be examined with respect to particular broadcast concerns, such as their reactions to the proposals of ACT and citizens' group participation in license renewal activities. Some commissioners have expressed their views on those matters publicly; others have not. One or two commissioners recently appointed to the FCC apparently have not had time to prepare themselves to form definite opinions. Following are the views of the commissioners who have formed and expressed opinions on those concerns when this investigation was undertaken. *

Former FCC Chairman Burch in a letter to the then Citizens Communication Center Director Albert Kramer said the FCC does not intend to discourage applicants in uncontested broadcast-license cases from paying "courtesy visits" to commissioners. Burch said informal communications by citizens' groups were "highly desirable," and indeed necessary to the functioning of an administrative agency such as the Commission. [64]

Burch said the WLBT-TV case, which opened the door to the controversy over access, established the right of even a single "affected" individual to intervene in a license-renewal proceeding. Even one person could have a valid complaint or a good idea. He said he felt citizens' group impact on broadcasting already has been great in terms of the changes in the law from court decisions. "By and large, this (the WLBT-TV decision) may be the scheme that was originally intended—more citizens playing a role in broadcasting. I don't think broadcasters welcome this." [65]

The former chairman also appointed a committee on administrative procedures, which was studying the possibility of the FCC pro-

_____

*Since this study was completed, Commissioners Johnson, H. Rex Lee, and Chairman Burch have left the commission. New commissioners are James Quello, Glen Robinson, and Abbott Washburn, whose views on this topic are not know.

viding public legal representatives for those who wish to oppose license renewal or redress other grievances.[66]

In a speech before the Arizona Broadcasters Association in 1970, Burch stated,

> When you sought the permit or license, you volunteered
> to serve as a public trustee or fiduciary—to make a reason-
> able, good faith effort to meet the needs and interests of
> your area. It follows that it is your obligation to listen
> to these community groups when they complain about
> that effort. . . . I do not mean to say or imply that you
> must accede to every request. A group may not be a
> responsible one or may not present worthwhile sugges-
> tions. . . . The Commission therefore welcomes the
> participation of responsible community groups in its
> licensing process. This is in line with the express
> statutory scheme and with the Court rulings that are
> squarely in point. We are taking steps to insure that
> the participation is fair and orderly—both to the com-
> munity groups and to the broadcasters. Our procedures
> are thus designed to afford a full and fair opportunity to
> the interested groups to participate and at the same time
> prevent disorderly, last minute requests for extension of
> time to file pleadings. . . . In sum, this trend of greater
> participation by community groups, is, I believe, a most
> significant development—and one which will not fade away.
> Responsible broadcasters should welcome it.[67]

Concerning ACT's request to ban commercials for youngsters and special programming for children, the commission, as noted earlier, did issue a notice of proposed rule-making inquiry. Burch said that broadcasters should not haggle over the number of children in the nation who may be affected adversely by programs with violence.

> Numbers aside, we simply do not believe that broadcasters
> should present children's programming in which violence
> is used as a deliberate device to grab onto a major share
> of the audience. They have no right—and I use the word
> advisedly—to put at risk any number of children to boost
> ratings. I think we're forced to ask whether traditional
> competition and the normal rules of the marketplace can
> really be left to operate in this area.[68]

He suggested that through joint consultation between networks, perhaps through the NAB, such improvements could be made, adding that such cooperation "would not be regarded as an antitrust violation by the Justice Department." Burch noted that the advertisers

> must give their whole-hearted support to the effort.
> More than support, they must exercise leadership
> and leverage. Advertisers cannot demand a good
> selling vehicle and then assume no responsibility
> for the quality of the product. They cannot criticize
> the present situation in children's television and then
> refuse to put their money in programs with appeal to
> specific age-groups, or in those that refuse to rely
> on violence as the way to build an audience. [69]

The ex-chairman told TV Guide he sensed a "lot of support" for ACT's proposal among his fellow commissioners, and, as a father, he was "sympathetic." However, he added, "I can't just be an advocate for my children and I'm not sure of the constitutionality of such rules. It's a very difficult case." [70] In a speech before the American Advertising Federation in February 1972, Burch said,

> Children are different. They cannot be treated like
> any other audience of potential customers. We make
> this distinction again and again. . . . I believe that in
> the case of advertising directed to children, the stand-
> ards of what is false and deceptive must be judged in
> light of the crucial fact that the audience is so unsophis-
> ticated, so young and trusting. It is, I submit, intolerable
> to seek to bilk the innocent with shoddy advertising appeals.
> As some person put it, that is akin to statutory rape.
>
> Either the industries involved—the advertiser and the
> broadcaster—take steps to correct the situation, or
> government will be called upon more and more fre-
> quently to take action. We have opened liaison with
> the Trade Commission on this matter. The problems
> will not go away. So my plea to you would be that any
> effective regulatory efforts commence here.

Burch said he has "called upon commercial broadcast leaders to make an all-out effort to develop TV programming which makes a positive contribution to the child's growth, his awareness of reality." [71]

Commissioner Robert E. Lee

Commissioner Robert E. Lee, who has been on the FCC since 1953, observed that "this is the age of the consumer. It's not as much fun being a broadcaster. If I were a broadcaster, I'd worry that someone might file against me and perhaps prevail." He suggested that broadcasters might wish to have their accountants carry a value of the station's network affiliation on the books in the event the license is lost to a challenger. [72]

Lee perceived the challenges to licenses as a major problem. "Certainly we'll be called upon to adjudicate more and more challenges to licenses." He told Television/Radio Age that broadcasters might wish to employ someone to look for the weak points of station operation and serve as a "devil's advocate" raising criticism that a challenger could use. He noted that "the day of maximum profits in broadcasting is gone," and suggested that licensees would do well to look toward protecting their franchises with "more and better programming and more attention to community needs." [73]

Lee advised broadcasters to seek legislation "which would take pressure off the FCC." But he suggested that licensees work out difficulties with community groups themselves without interference by the FCC. He regarded community group challenges to license renewals as basically a matter of "good relations in the community and attentiveness to needs." [74]

Regarding children's programming, Lee predicted more FCC intrusion into such programming. "I don't think I am capable of saying what is good for children's programming. . . . This investigation (by the commission regarding ACT's proposals) is going to the very heart of potential censorship." [75]

Commissioner H. Rex Lee

Former Commissioner H. Rex Lee, who has been on the commission since 1968, observed that the most immediate problems faced by the broadcast industry are license-renewal policy, the public's increasing demand for access to the broadcast media, and the "wholesale criticism of current programming efforts," according to an interview with Television/Radio Age. In the interview he expressed concern and discouragement with the

> basic sameness of the industry, the overriding preoccupation with ratings and revenues and with the reluctance of broadcasters to deal with social problems.

He has noted that the future of the industry is dependent on "its ability to engage the listening and viewing public in a way that will inspire only nobler desires and motives."

Commissioner Lee emphasized that it is "not enough that a broadcaster grudgingly agree to reduce the number of commercials during children's programming." The broadcaster must assume "his basic responsibility for effecting a social change. . . . he must return the innovative spirit that characterized the pioneering periods in radio and television in an earnest effort to re-establish a belief in, and a respect for, the basic values of our democracy."[76]

Commissioner Charlotte T. Reid

Charlotte T. Reid, former member of the House of Representatives, was appointed to the FCC in 1971. She acknowledged that the license renewal area was a "major matter" for commission action. She also expressed concern about children's programming as both a mother and a grandmother. She noted that the biggest challenge faced by broadcasters was being responsive to the needs and desires of the audience.

However, Commissioner Reid favors deregulation of both radio and television, as opposed to more regulation. The success of regulation depends on the extent to which industry meets its challenges, according to a trade journal interview with her.[77]

Apparently since taking office she has not issued many public statements or taken key positions in policy decisions, although she could assume a more active role on the commission.

Commissioner Richard E. Wiley

Commissioner Richard E. Wiley is also a recent appointee to the FCC. He joined the commission in 1971, although he had been its general counsel since 1970. He became chairman in 1973.

Wiley stated,

With regard to my personal views, I most assuredly believe that local citizens councils can be beneficial to the public and useful to licensees in the ascertain-

ment of community needs. Members of the public,
no less than broadcast licensees and indeed, the
Commission itself, are responsible for improving
upon our system of broadcasting. That has also
been the Commission's consistent policy, at least
since the release of the "Blue Book" in 1946. Of
course we have come a long way since our passing
reference to such councils in the summary of that
Report. Our recent release of a pamphlet entitled
"The Public and Broadcasting—A Procedural Manual"
is indicative of the Commission's continuing interest
in promoting public participation in the administrative
process.[78]

His views of that manual were described earlier in this chapter.

The chairman indicated earlier that he regarded the threat of
license challenges as a major issue in broadcasting. He noted that
the threat of challenges based only on promises and the policy of
awarding a demerit to licensees with other communications interests
may "drive some of the best people out of the broadcasting business."
He said that constant license challenges would lead to "exactly the
opposite of what the people attacking the licensees are seeking."[79]

Chairman Wiley said there should be reasonable assurances of
license renewal to the broadcaster who is "supplying good-faith,
strong, solid service to his community." He approved the FCC's revised primer on ascertaining community needs, but believes the broadcaster should have some discretion on how to meet community needs.
He pointed out that the FCC should review its standards to see if it
has been arbitrary.

He approved the recent FCC decision to renew the license of
WMAL-TV and of the United States Court of Appeals' affirmation of
that decision. He said the court's decision was a "reaffirmation of
the Commission's belief that responsible and diligent licensee effort
is the industry's best safeguard at renewal time." The station's license was under challenge from a citizens' group that charged that
it had failed to ascertain adequately community needs and failed to
provide programming of interest for the local black community. Wiley
said that decision "goes a long way toward insuring the Commission's traditional policy of permitting broadcasters wide discretion
in programming, community needs ascertainment and equal employment."[80]

Commissioner Nicholas Johnson

The views of former Commissioner Nicholas Johnson have been stated in previous chapters. As commissioner he gave a number of speeches and was a prolific writer. He has written numerous articles and one book, which have expressed his philosophy toward broadcasting and the FCC. A believer in participatory democracy, the former commissioner urged that citizens and citizens' groups should involve themselves more in broadcast problems and policy.

Indeed, the proceeds from his book, How to Talk Back to Your Television Set, help support the Stern Community Law Firm, a citizens' group offering legal expertise to private and other citizens' organizations. [81] He also suggested that national citizens' action groups be formed to assist the FCC and that the commission establish a legal aid bureau to assist the public. [82]

Commissioner Benjamin L. Hooks

Commissioner Benjamin L. Hooks is one of the three newer members of the FCC (he joined in June 1972). In the short period he has been on the commission, Hooks has expressed interest in citizens' groups involved in broadcasting, particularly from the point of view of how stations have served local minority groups.

In an interview with a trade publication, Commissioner Hooks stated, "I am a 'law and order man' when it comes to enforcement of the government's regulations regarding hiring and promotion without discrimination against minorities or women." He said he hoped to be involved with the FCC's committee that determines equal employment opportunities standards for stations. Regarding programming, Commissioner Hooks noted, "The larger white community doesn't get a balanced picture of what Black folks are about, and it just seems to me that this is one of the jobs that television has to do." He apparently considered it fundamental for broadcasters to operate in the public interest and acknowledged their right to earn a profit sumultaneously. He feels stations sometimes simply do not have enough hours to serve properly the interests of all communities. The trade journal noted, "It is certain he will not go along with pro forma license renewal of stations that do not appear to be meeting the requirements for affirmative action in hiring minorities. 'I will not be mollified by token or partial adherence to the regulations.' "[83]

Commissioner Hooks wrote,

> In regard to your various questions on citizens councils,
> the Commission has always required broadcasters to
> serve the tastes, needs and interests of its community
> of license. A licensee has many avenues in ascertaining
> these needs and interests, but the Commission has de-
> termined that one of the better avenues is through con-
> sultation with community leaders. Leaders from local
> citizens groups, such as labor, business, educational
> and minority groups, etc., may reflect the community's
> tastes and needs, and as such would be a prime source
> of information for licensees. The Commission's concern
> in this regard is reflected in the application forms of
> broadcast applicants. [84]

In October 1972, Commissioner Hooks dissented to the FCC's
decision to renew the licenses of 11 Omaha, Nebraska, radio and
television stations. The stations' renewal applications had been opposed by an organization of local blacks, the Black Identity Educational
Association (BIEA) on grounds of discriminatory employment practices
and failure of providing programming that met the needs of that
group. [85]

In his dissenting opinion Hooks stated, "Somebody, some day
soon, must get to the source of Black disaffection with the media. . . .
Omaha is a good place as any to start. . . . Sharing the concern of
the minority groups across this land for a better shake from the
government, at a minimum, I would have looked deeper into the pro-
testations of BIEA."[86]

Commissioner Hooks' concern apparently has been directed
toward how broadcasters can best serve minority groups, although
his interests may not be restricted to that direction.

THE COURTS

In addition to the FCC and the White House Office of Telecommunications Policy, there is yet another government vehicle that has
influenced both broadcasting and the FCC: the United States Court
of Appeals for the District of Columbia. On occasion, the United
States Supreme Court has ruled on decisions affecting broadcast
matters, but the highest court does so only by upholding or reversing
the decisions of lower courts. And the United States Court of Appeals
is the court to which affected parties may turn when FCC decisions
are not considered appropriate.

Broadcasting in 1971 said this court "with dizzying regularity, has reversed the Commission on most issues of importance to come before it in recent years." The trade journal further states the court has effected two basic and related transformations in broadcast regulations. The first decision was, as noted earlier, reversing the traditional concept of "legal standing," which provides public interest groups—citizens' groups—opportunity to intervene in license renewal proceedings. The second decision centered on the concept of "fairness."[87] Previously the broadcaster had nearly "unlimited discretion in handling of controversial issues." In ruling that broadcasters who sell time for commercials may not, as a matter of policy, refuse to sell time for the broadcast of opinion, it extended the fairness doctrine.

The United States Court of Appeals within the last decade has overturned—and upheld—a number of decisions of the FCC. The WLBT-TV decision has been described previously, although it should be noted that the court severely chastised the commission. The court, under then Judge Warren E. Burger, told the FCC,

> The examiner and the Commission exhibited at best a
> reluctant tolerance of this court's mandate and at worst
> a profound hostility to the participation of the public-
> interest intervenors and their efforts. . . .the admin-
> istrative conduct reflected in this record is beyond
> repair.[88]

In another decision, the court overturned the FCC's 1970 statement on license renewal policy, which held that no competing application for a broadcast facility would be accepted if the incumbent licensee could demonstrate he had performed "substantial service." The court ruled the commission had violated the Communications Act by denying a hearing to qualified applicants. Broadcast critic Shayon observed the court has

> forthrightly reminded the FCC that it isn't doing its job
> and ought to get on with it—restoring competition of broad-
> casting, opening the door to minority ownership of stations,
> breaking up monopolies, and defining and rewarding superior
> service. The message is loud and clear.[89]

In August 1968, the court said the FCC should have granted legal standing to a citizens' group seeking to block the sale of WFMT (FM), Chicago, and implied that a hearing should have been held. And in October 1970, the court held that the commission should have held hearings on the protests of citizens' groups against the transfer of classical music stations WGKA AM-FM, Atlanta, Georgia.[90]

In a decision more favorable to the FCC cited earlier, the court upheld the commission's decision to renew the license of WMAL-TV, Washington, D.C. The decision could have a significant impact on citizens' groups. In that case, the petition had been filed by 16 black leaders stating the station had failed to serve the program needs of the area, which has a 70 percent black population. The FCC, in denying the petition, said the station had surveyed the black community adequately, and that the programming percentages were commensurate with the area's black population. [91]

Broadcasting stated that the court's decision "probably means the Commission will be less inclined to set protested renewals for hearings that it would otherwise." The journal noted that some 100 renewals on the commission's deferred list have filed protests and petitions similar to those contained in the petition filed against WMAL-TV. The trade journal said in an editorial that the "decision shortens the odd confrontations between challengers and licensees" and welcomes the ruling. The editorial added that broadcasters should not neglect "its work on the bills it has been supporting" to protect broadcast licensees from future challenges. [92]

Saturday Review columnist Shayon noted in 1971,

the consumer movement in broadcasting has reached a gut issue—the relationship of programming to profits. The surfacing of the issue of discovery (which followed the older issue of the right of citizen groups to intervene in renewal cases) is both a symptom of this new problem and a sign of progress. The FCC apparently still considers citizens' groups as hostile. The opportunity then is once again in the corner of that perceptive and spirited Court of Appeals for the District of Columbia.

Shayon noted that the court since 1969 has encouraged citizens to "take an active interest in the scope and quality of the television service."[93]

Referring to the FCC's denial of the Alianza Federal de Pueblos Libres' request to have access to the annual financial reports of KGGM-TV, Albuquerque, New Mexico, Shayon said the FCC "stood as a shield before the Albuquerque stations, even though neither the Commission nor the stations in any way indicated how they could be hurt by public disclosure of their financial reports."[94]

OFFICE OF TELECOMMUNICATIONS POLICY

There is yet another government office concerned with the problems of broadcasting and with FCC policy: the Office of Telecommunications Policy of the Executive Office of the President. The office in

1973 was directed by Clay T. Whitehead who was also an adviser to
President Richard Nixon on communications matters. Henry Goldberg,
office counsel and assistant to Whitehead, in 1972 stated,

> With respect to citizens' councils, we have not had the
> occasion to study their antecedents or take a position on
> the desirability of the local council as a means of strength-
> ening the broadcasters' ties to their communities. We have,
> however, strongly supported the general principle that the
> broadcast licensee must be responsive to the needs and in-
> terests of his service area—the principle that also underlies
> the council concept. We feel that licensees should be re-
> quired to fulfill their public service responsibilities through
> ascertainment of community needs, interests, problems and
> issues, and by responding through their programming.

> With respect to Action for Children's Television (ACT)
> and the WLBT case, both broadly speaking are instances
> of the formal citizen participation in the broadcast reg-
> ulatory process necessary to broadcasting's realizing
> its full potential. When combined with the informal
> citizen involvement in broadcasting through ascertain-
> ment, the WLBT case's removal of barriers to direct
> citizen group participation in FCC processes will facil-
> itate a continuing infusion of new ideas and new concepts
> of public service into the broadcast industry. The ACT
> petition and the FCC proceeding it prompted, are, per-
> haps, the best recent examples of how citizen groups
> can get results by using the orderly processes of the
> FCC.

> As with any right, however, the right of citizen groups
> to have a say in determining the type of broadcast service
> made available by the licensees must be exercised with
> responsibility. There have been, for example, instances
> of the right of participation being used by individual groups
> solely for the purpose of furthering their own self-interest.
> This is the type of problem that can be worked out as we
> gain more experience with the relatively new forms of
> public involvement in the broadcast media. The appropriate
> form and extent of citizen participation are matters that
> should be determined within the larger context of govern-
> ment regulatory policy as a whole. We have taken the view
> that, in order to obtain programming that is substantially
> attuned to community and audience needs, several basic

reforms in current policy must be effectuated in the
areas of the Fairness Doctrine, access to the media,
and licensing procedures. [95]

In a speech delivered to the Ohio Association of Broadcasters
at Columbus, Ohio, on September 29, 1971, Whitehead said many
problems in broadcasting have centered around the 1934 Communications Act.

Despite all the bitterness engendered by specific access
disputes, as evidenced by the license challenges right
here in Columbus, and other Ohio cities, you should
recognize that your critics are doing nothing more
than seeking more effective and practical means of
achieving the intended results of the Communications
Act. It's fruitless to argue at this late stage that the
intent of the Act has been perverted. Times change—
this is the way it is now. If you don't like it, either
change the Act or find a line of business where there's
no Communications Act and a public committed enough
to tell you what its interest is. [96]

Whitehead appeared to be keenly aware of the problems involved
in license renewals and of citizens groups. He stated,

No matter how the renewal challenges are resolved in
Columbus and elsewhere, the process of redefining the
broadcasters' relationship with the various publics to
be served is just beginning. This painful and difficult
process can proceed as it has begun. It can go on city-
by-city in an atmosphere of mutual distrust, emotional
blood-letting and even fear, or it can be recognized for
the critical policy problem it is and approached in a
manner that does not pit broadcasters and citizens in a
battle that both view as essential to their survival. No
progress can be made when local broadcasters and local
citizens groups see themselves as adversaries—this is
the ultimate perversion of the intent of the Communications Act—from public trustee to public enemy. We've
got to go back and work out a new relationship between
the licensee and the public before this goes much further.

We must address ourselves to these basic flaws that are
all too apparent in our broadcast regulation, especially
the structural flaws that developed in our public access
mechanisms. [97]

In a speech in October 1971, before the International Radio and Television Society, Whitehead proposed the elimination of the fairness doctrine and a change in the license renewal process. Regarding the abolishing of the fairness doctrine, he suggested,

> It should be replaced by an Act of Congress that provides
> for both the rights of individuals to speak, and the need
> of the public at large to receive coverage of public issues.
> There are two distinct claims, and they cannot both be
> served by the same mechanism.

He suggested that television time be

> set aside for sale to be made available on a first-come,
> first-served basis at nondiscriminatory rates but there
> must be no rate regulation. The individual would have
> a right to speak on any matter, whether it's to sell razor
> blades or urge an end to the war. This private right of
> access should be enforced—as most private rights are
> enforced—through the courts, and not through the FCC. [98]

Concerning his second proposal involving a change in the license renewal process, Whitehead stated,

> There should be a longer TV license period, with the
> license revocable for cause. The FCC would invite or
> entertain competing applications only when a license
> is not renewed or is revoked. To assure the right of
> the public to be informed on public issues, the licensee
> would be obligated to make the totality of programming
> that is under his control (including PSA's) responsive
> to the interests and concerns of the community.
>
> The criterion for renewal would be whether the broad-
> caster has, over the term of his license, made a good
> faith effort to ascertain the needs and interests of his
> community and to meet them in his programming. There
> would be no place in the renewal process for government-
> conceived program categories, percentages, formats, or
> any value judgment on specific program content.
>
> I believe these revisions in the access and renewal pro-
> cesses will add stability to your industry, and avoid the
> bitter adversary struggle between you and your community
> groups. They recognize the new concerns of access and
> fairness in a way that minimizes government content control. [99]

These points also were stressed by Whitehead in his December 18, 1972, speech cited in Chapter 1.

In sum, it appears that the Office of Telecommunications Policy (OTP) sought to encourage both public participation and station responsibility to community interests and needs. The OTP also sought to stabilize the broadcast industry and avoid the "adversary struggle" in which community groups are pitted against the stations. Without describing specific details in his proposals, Whitehead believed when he was in office that the television license periods should be lengthened. This was in line with the NAB-supported proposed legislation in Congress.

Whether Whithead's successor, who has yet to be named, will take an active stance in commercial broadcasting remains to be seen.

THE WHITE HOUSE

To indicate the extent to which government officials regard the importance of citizens' groups challenging license renewals, former President Nixon in June 1972 invited and met with 30 executives of the major broadcast companies. Included in the discussion was the topic of license challenges. According to one account, the broadcasters "heard a very friendly President tell them how concerned he was with their problems."[100]

The following month, representatives of citizens' groups and lawyers who have represented them wrote the president requesting that they too should have an audience with him. Their request stated that since the president sought the views of the broadcasters concerning challenges to license renewals, the White House should offer "equal time" to them. The groups included representatives from Action for Children's Television, Citizens Communications Center, The United Church of Christ, Black Efforts for Soul in Television, the National Organization for Women, the Stern Community Law Firm, and others.[101]

Their letter said they sought to counter what they felt was the broadcasters' argument that license-renewal challenges constitute a threat to the industry's "stability and profitability." The message noted that "no more than two or three broadcasters have lost their licenses as a result of citizen participation" and that the effect of citizen participation has been the establishment of a dialogue between the broadcasters and his community, which "permits previously disenfranchised segments of the society to participate in controlling the media's impact on their lives." Their request also noted that such participation in the regulatory process not only results from

"the failure of broadcasters generally to tailor their broadcast operations to local concerns," but "has been condoned and approved
by the courts. . . . Just as the regulatory processes must reflect
divergent viewpoints, so too must there be opportunity for different
perspectives to be directly heard at the presidential level."[102] The
White House did not reply to their request.

President Gerald Ford's administration's attitude toward broadcasting and consumerism remains unclear. In October 1974 he did
propose a commission to study the regulatory agencies with the view
of improving the efficiency of those bodies.

THE PUBLIC

One further point regarding reactions to citizens' groups needs
to be discussed: the attitude of the general public toward citizens'
councils and participatory democracy applied to commercial broadcasting.

The question of who speaks for the public was raised in Chapter
1, in which it was pointed out that no one group could speak for the
public and that there are many publics. The same answer could be
applied to how the general public perceives and regards citizens'
groups.

This survey has attempted to trace available information involving citizens' groups. Nearly all such references concerning
citizens' councils directly or indirectly were in publications relating
to law, consumer interest, the field of broadcasting, government
documents, or academic journals. No reference was located that
examined general public attitudes toward citizens' groups.

Perhaps the only in-depth study that investigated general public
attitudes toward television was Gary Steiner's The People Look at
Television.[103] One of his findings indicated that the people would
rather the broadcast industry "clean itself" rather than having an
audience screen programs before such programs were aired. Conceivably, that observation could be interpreted to indicate the public
does not wish to become involved, but such an interpretation would
be hazardous. And Steiner's study did not examine the area of public
participation or the public's attitudes toward citizens' groups. The
same limitation applies to a 1973 study, Television and the Public by
Robert T. Bower, which attempts to replicate Steiner's investigation.[104]

Other studies involving public attitudes toward radio were The
People Look at Radio (1946)[105] and Radio Listening in America
(1948),[106] both by Paul Lazarsfeld and others. All three studies were

supported by the NAB. Lazarsfeld's studies did not examine the public's views toward citizens' councils or participatory democracy in
broadcasting. Beyond these studies little exists.

Until such an investigation specifically pursuing general public
attitudes is conducted, any assumptions or generalizations involving
public reactions would be unsubstantiated. It could be speculated,
however, that since most people who participate in voluntary associations tend to come from the middle class, those in the other strata
probably would be less inclined to become involved. And lack of involvement probably would indicate indifference, lack of concern, or
apathy toward citizens' groups and participatory democracy.

THE IMPACT OF CITIZENS' GROUPS AND THE FCC

The question could be asked, what do all the above-mentioned
activities mean? Have they had any impact on the broadcast industry?
Ancil Payne, general manager of King Broadcasting Corporation in
Seattle, and a member of the board of directors of the NAB has stated,
"There is no doubt but that broadcasters have been under more relent-
less and varying forms of attack and pressure by this (President
Nixon's) administration than ever before." He stated, "Some of these
pressures like determining community needs or opening access to programming to all elements within the community or recognizing minority
employment needs are completely warranted." He added he was opposed to "forced counter-advertising, the preoccupation with minutiae
regarding licensing, and the willingness to be blackmailed."[107]

From a different perspective, Television/Radio Age in a survey
of 200 television stations reported that the average station has increased locally originated programming during 1972. The trade journal
reported that the "average TV station aired 16 hours and 18 minutes
of locally-produced programming a week during the survey period,
which was late June. This compared with 15 hours and 36 minutes
in last year's survey, taken during a corresponding period." The
journal noted that the FCC's prime time access rule was "largely
responsible" for this increase; but there were other factors including
"license renewal obligations and challenges, community pressure,
competition, and an honest desire to serve their viewers."[108]

The commission's issuing of the "how-to-do-it" manual described earlier tends to support the view that the FCC encourages

broadcast licensees and citizens' groups to settle their differences privately without commission action or interference.

In summary, the FCC was indeed cognizant of citizens' groups, but it appeared reluctant to offer such groups total support. This also seemed to be the view of the individual commissioners and of Whitehead. Each seemed to feel that if citizens' groups can help the broadcaster become more responsive to the needs of his community, such groups could be beneficial. In other words, citizens' groups are only one vehicle by which broadcast stations can ascertain or determine community interests. And if licensees are able to operate their stations in an efficient and equitable manner without citizens' groups, the commission would not object.

The courts, however, appeared to have been more sympathetic to citizens' groups. As noted earlier, the United States Court of Appeals reversed an FCC decision and awarded legal standing to a citizens' group. The same court also reversed the FCC's 1970 license renewal policy statement. But it should also be noted that the United States Court of Appeals has on occasion upheld FCC decisions in which citizens' group requests were denied.

At this point, we next examine three case studies of representative citizens' groups in Chapter 5.

NOTES

1. U.S., Federal Communications Commission, The FCC in Fiscal 1971 (Washington, D.C.: Government Printing Office, 1972), p. 9.

2. "Inside The FCC," Television/Radio Age, June 14, 1971, p. 59.

3. "Inside The FCC," Television/Radio Age, February 22, 1971, p. 77.

4. CPB Report, Weekly Newsletter of Corporation for Public Broadcasting 5 No. 35 (September 1974): 1.

5. Ibid.

6. "Bad Case of Nerves Develops Over Alabama Situation," Broadcasting, September 30, 1974, pp. 23-4.

7. Les Brown, Television, The Business Behind the Box (New York: Harcourt, Brace, Jovanovich, 1971), p. 179.

8. Robert Coase, "The Economics of Broadcasting and Public Policy," cited in Paul MacAvoy, ed., The Crisis of the Regulatory Commissions (New York: W. W. Norton, 1970), p. 95.

9. Marcus Cohn, "Should The FCC Reward Stations That Do a Good Job," Saturday Review, August 14, 1971, p. 45.

10. Frank Kahn, Documents of American Broadcasting (New York: Appleton-Century-Crofts, 1968), pp. 197-8.

11. O. Joe Olson, ed., Education On The Air (Columbus: Ohio State University Press, 1950), pp. 361-2.

12. Ibid., p. 363.

13. Ibid.

14. Charles Siepmann, Radio, Television and Society (New York: Oxford University Press, 1960), p. 37.

15. The Center For The Study of Democratic Instituions, Broadcasting and Government Regulation in a Free Society (Santa Barbara: The Center For The Study of Democratic Institutions, 1959), p. 7.

16. Ibid., p. 26.

17. Ibid.

18. Meyer Weinberg, TV In America (New York: Ballantine Books, 1962), p. 113.

19. Kahn, op. cit., p. 218.

20. Weinberg op. cit., p. 276.

21. U.S., Federal Communications Commission, The FCC in Fiscal 1969, Annual Report, pp. 18-20.

22. "Relief is Just a Senate Bill Away," Broadcasting, October 11, 1971, p. 48.

23. "WWJ-TV, WTCJ Renewed," Broadcasting, June 5, 1972, p. 10.

24. "Two After-Deadline File Petitions," Broadcasting, December 6, 1971, p. 30.

25. "At FCC: More Aid to Challengers?," Broadcasting, July 5, 1971, p. 47.

26. "Settling In: Mrs. Roberts and Dr. Pearce," Broadcasting, October 4, 1971, p. 36.

27. New York Times article in The Oregonian, October 14, 1974.

28. Ibid.

29. Ibid.

30. "The Struggle Over Broadcast Access," Broadcasting, September 20, 1971, p. 17.

31. Nicholas Johnson, speech delivered to the International Association of Political Consultants, London, England, December 14, 1970.

32. U.S., Federal Communications Commission. "Primer on Ascertainment of Community Problems by Broadcast Applicants" in Federal Register 36 No. 42 (March 3, 1971).

33. U.S., Federal Communications Commission, 39th Annual Report/Fiscal Year 1973, pp. 67-8.

34. "FCC Issues Its New Rules for Program Reporting," Broadcasting, May 7, 1973, pp. 28-30.

35. Ibid.

36. The Oregonian, July 24, 1972.

37. Ibid.

38. Robert Lewis Shayon, "Act with ACT," Saturday Review, March 7, 1970, p. 22.

39. "30 Stations Queried on Employment Records," Broadcasting, July 31, 1972, p. 37.

40. Ibid.

41. "Inside the FCC," Television/Radio Age, March 8, 1971, pp. 61-2.

42. Ibid.

43. U.S., Federal Communications Commission, The Public and Broadcasting in Federal Register, Part III 37, No. 190 (September 29, 1972): 20518.

44. Letter from Commissioner Richard E. Wiley, October 12, 1972.

45. "Compensation to Challenges: Blackmail or Part of the Process?," Broadcasting, September 18, 1972, p. 24.

46. Ibid.

47. Ibid.

48. U.S., Federal Communications Commission, Notice of Inquiry and Notice of Proposed Rule Making, Docket 18859, May 18, 1970.

49. Donald Gillmore, and Jerome Barron, Supplement to Mass Communication Law (St. Paul: West Publishing Co., 1971), pp. 223-4.

50. "Seven NAB-Type Bills Are Now in The House," Broadcasting, January 31, 1972, p. 19.

51. "Broadcasters Win One at the High Court," Broadcasting, June 4, 1973, pp. 22-3.

52. "Inside the FCC," Television/Radio Age, June 25, 1973, pp. 87-8.

53. Ibid., p. 87.

54. "Flat Ban on Reimbursement Vetoed," Broadcasting, April 3, 1972, p. 117.

55. "How Much Too Much in Reimbursing Challengers? FCC Wants to Know", Broadcasting, June 5, 1972, p. 34.

56. Robert Lewis Shayon, "Fairness Deferred," Saturday Review, April 29, 1972, p. 23.

57. Marcus Cohn, "Should the FCC Reward Stations That Do a Good Job?", Saturday Review, August 14, 1971, p. 45.

58. "Bartley Looks Back At His 20 Years From FCC Doorway," Broadcasting, June 26, 1972, p. 34.

59. "The Texarkana Agreement as a Model Strategy for Citizen Participation in FCC License Renewals," Harvard Journal on Legislation 17, No. 4 (May 1970): 633-634.

60. Ibid.

61. U.S., Federal Communications Commission, FCC letter to station KTAL-TV, FCC69-827, July 29, 1969.

62. U.S., Federal Communications Commission, statement by Commissioner Nicholas Johnson accompanying FCC letter to station KTAL-TV, July 29, 1969.

63. Sydney Head, Broadcasting in America (Boston: Houghton Mifflin Co., 1972), p. 524.

64. "Burch: Welcome Mat Always Out At FCC," Broadcasting, January 10, 1972, p. 47.

65. "The Struggle Over Broadcast Access (II)," Broadcasting, September 27, 1971, p. 26.

66. Television/Radio Age, June 14, 1971, p. 60.

67. "Inside the FCC," Television/Radio Age, March 22, 1971, p. 98.

68. "Inside the FCC," Television/Radio Age, April 3, 1972, p. 55.

69. Ibid.

70. "Boston Tea Party-1970," TV Guide, July 4, 1970, p. 14.

71. Dean Burch, speech delivered to the American Advertising Federation, Washington, D.C., February 2, 1971.

72. Television/Radio Age, April 3, 1972, op. cit., p. 58.

73. Television/Radio Age, February 22, 1971, op. cit., p. 78.

74. Ibid., p. 58.

75. Ibid., p. 77.

76. Television/Radio Age, April 3, 1972, op. cit., pp. 62-3.

77. Ibid.

78. Wiley letter, October 12, 1972, op. cit.

79. Television/Radio Age, April 3, 1972, op. cit., p. 62.

80. "Wiley Likes WMAL Decision," Broadcasting, July 17, 1972, p. 32.

81. Broadcasting, September 20, 1971, op. cit., p. 36.

82. Nicholas Johnson, How To Talk Back To Your Television Set (New York: Bantam Books, 1970), p. 36.

83. "Inside the FCC," Television/Radio Age, August 21, 1972, pp. 75-6.

84. Letter from Commissioner Benjamin Hooks, September 27, 1972.

85. "Hooks Starts Delivering on His Commitment to Blacks," Broadcasting, October 9, 1972, p. 31.

86. Ibid.

87. "Broadcasting's Pre-emptive Court," Broadcasting, August 30, 1971, p. 17.

88. Ibid.

89. Robert Lewis Shayon, "Collision Course," Saturday Review, August 7, 1971, p. 38.

90. Broadcasting, August 30, 1971, op. cit., p. 19.

91. "Court Backs FCC on WMAL Renewal," Broadcasting, July 3, 1972, p. 6.

92. "Hear, Hear," Broadcasting, July 10, 1972, p. 60.

93. Robert Shayon, "Chickens and Foxes," Saturday Review, October 16, 1971, p. 73.

94. Ibid.

95. Letter from Henry Goldberg, August 24, 1972.

96. Clay Whitehead, speech delivered to Ohio Association of Broadcasters, Columbus, Ohio, September 29, 1971.

97. Ibid.

98. Clay Whitehead, speech delivered to International Radio and Television Society, New York, New York, October 6, 1971.

99. Ibid.

100. Oregon Journal, July 28, 1972.

101. "Other Side Tries For Nixon's Ear," Broadcasting, July 24, 1972, p. 62.

102. Ibid., p. 63.

103. Gary Steiner, The People Look at Television: A Study of Audience Attitudes (New York: Alfred A. Knopf, 1963), p. 26.

104. Robert T. Bower, Television and The Public (New York: Holt, Rinehart and Winston, 1973).

105. Paul Lazarsfeld and Harry Field, The People Look at Radio (Chapel Hill: University of North Carolina Press, 1946).

106. Paul Lazarsfeld and Patricia Kendall, Radio Listening in America: The People Look at Radio Again (New York: Prentice-Hall, 1948).

107. Oregon Journal, July 28, 1972.

108. "Access Rule Increases Station Originations," Television/ Radio Age, July 24, 1972, pp. 21-4.

5

THREE CITIZENS'
GROUPS

Participation increases feedback; it encourages learning
and adjustment as experience is gained with new politics.
It compels the recognition of diversity.

Allen Altschuler

As mentioned earlier, there are several types of citizens'
groups. One is the community group having long range goals for broadcast programs in an area involving all local stations. This group is
established on a permanent basis. Such an example would be the Greater
Cleveland (Ohio) Radio and Television Council. A second type of citizens' organization is a group formed on a national basis to influence
the FCC, individual stations, and the national networks. Action for
Children's Television is such an example. A third form includes
organizations that provide specific expertise and legal advice to various
local groups on a nonprofit basis. For this category, Citizens Communications Center will be cited.

This section will examine those three groups as representative
citizens' organizations. This selection and categorization is not designed to be comprehensive and definitive. Other categories and examples could be cited. The three groups have been selected because
it is hoped that by using them as examples of citizens' organizations,
students of broadcasting, broadcasters, and government agencies
could learn from their experiences. Because of the manner in which
each of these groups has operated, one an organization with long range
goals, another with action-oriented purposes, and the third a specialized organization, each provides an example of a differing style of
operation. Yet all are concerned with commercial broadcasting and
with the manner in which broadcasters have served their communities.

They were different but similar, and at times their goals overlapped. All have been active in broadcast matters. The Cleveland group has been praised by the FCC; ACT has been aggressive in trying to alter children's programming; and the Citizens Communications Center has been criticized by broadcasting.

THE GREATER CLEVELAND RADIO
AND TELEVISION COUNCIL

The Greater Cleveland Radio and Television Council was one of the citizens' groups most often mentioned in the literature of broadcasting as an exemplary council. The FCC cited the Cleveland council as "outstanding,"[1] and Charles Siepmann described it as a precedent "for all to emulate."[2] The council has existed in a metropolitan area of 2,064,194 population in which there are five AM and 13 AM and FM radio stations and six television stations.[3]

Founded in 1940, the Cleveland broadcast council in 1972 had a total membership of 163, including 42 individual members and 121 representatives from other organizations. The organization's members represent "PTA's, PTU's, civic, cultural, church-affiliated groups and broadcasting media."[4] Mrs. A. J. Matkovick, 1970 president of the council, wrote,

> Basically, our Council is an educational organization. We try to serve as a coordinating body between the public and the broadcasters. We inform our members on evaluation, rights and responsibilities of the citizen and the broadcaster, how and where to register complaints, etc.

> Our relationship with broadcasters has been congenial. We are called on in the area of ascertainment. They are most cooperative in providing speakers on various aspects of the industry.

> This 1970-71 year began the first year of a three-year study dealing exclusively with Cleveland-area stations. We are aiming to learn as much as we can about them and their service to the community as it affects license renewals. As far as we know, there are no other Councils such as ours. . . . We think other cities should have such organizations.

Perhaps we have survived because we have tried to
change with the times. Perhaps due to the foundation
on which we were built. We do have a firm nucleus of
members whose interest seems to carry us along.
More people do seem to be involved with television
viewing than with radio listening which is understandable when the family is considered. We have tried to
expand our work with radio evaluation this year.[5]

The council began to form in 1938 when several women's cultural
clubs formed radio study groups.

Among them were the Olla Podrida Club, the Federation
of Women's Clubs and the Cleveland Colony of the National Society of New England Women. On September
12, 1940, Miss Julia Fish and Mrs. Laura Goodhue,
representing the New England Women, invited members
of various organizations whose natural concerns might
well include the improvement of radio programs to attend
a meeting of the Cleveland Colony at which radio programs
for children and the work of Radio Councils then springing
up in various sections of the country were discussed.[6]

During the group's first year, a program evaluation committee
was organized under the leadership of William B. Levenson, who
established a method of evaluating radio programs. (Levenson at
that time was on the Cleveland Board of Education and subsequently
became superintendent of schools in Cleveland.) In September 1941,
a two-day regional conference was held and representatives of 19
nearby cities attended. Subsequent conferences were held for several
years.
        The Cleveland group received some impetus from Robert Stephan,
radio editor of the Cleveland Plain Dealer. Llewellyn White in 1947
noted that the council

confines its efforts to Greater Cleveland, claims to
speak for 155,000; conducts occasionally door-to-door,
mail and telephone surveys, and publishes periodic
"evaluative" program lists. Like the (Better Radio
Listening Council of) Wisconsin group, it bars anyone
connected with the industry from membership or active
participation.[7]

According to the council's regulations, the group meets monthly September through May. Twenty-five members constitute a quorum. It has 14 committees, which include those of evaluation, membership, public relations, and so on. Its constitution states the responsibilities of the evaluation committees in both radio and television shall be to have as large a representation as possible in Greater Cleveland, to listen to and view programs according to prescribed standards, and to be objective in their evaluation. All (broadcast) programs shall be considered three times before presentation to the executive board for final approval for <u>Selective Dialing</u>. [8] (This is a 20-page printed publication listing stations and programs selected for commendation.)

Concerning membership dues, the council's rules state, "The annual cooperating member's fees shall be as follows: Organizations, $7.00, individual, $5.00, sustaining individual, $10.00 or more, sustaining organizational, $25.00, or more."[9]

The Council issues a 3 x 5-inch folded brochure, "Guidelines for Evaluating Radio and Television Programs," which is based on the Radio Code of Good Practices and the Television Code of the National Association of Broadcasters. The organization also issues a monthly bulletin announcing radio and television programs described as "specials" to be viewed and heard by local members. Broadcast awards are presented each year. There are six categories of awards: children's programs, community service and public affairs, news, entertainment, religious, and commercial. [10]

In addition to evaluating programs, the council makes a serious effort to understand broadcasting and the problems of broadcasters. In the spring of 1972, the council adopted a "Take a Broadcaster to Lunch" program. The program was originated by Clare Bartunek, council president. [11] In March 1972, Bartunek described the council.

> We have tried to represent the people at home—not
> as statistics but as living loving parents and children
> whose lives are fashioned, in part, by what they see
> and hear on the air. We have tried to be public voice
> with annual critical comments, annual awards of com-
> mendation and frequent public discussions. [12]

The Cleveland Council has taken the initiative in terms of attempting to improve or change both network and local programming. It has undertaken constructive attempts to understand commercial broadcasting and to cooperate with local stations by providing broadcast materials and personnel. Council members have circulated and signed petitions.

In the past, we have cooperated by request with
national radio and TV organizations by having
petitions circulated and sent to the network to
continue the program "Captain Kangaroo" on the
national network.

Last year we filed a petition to the FCC supporting
the "ACT" Group in their drive to bring about reform
in childrens' TV programming on commercial television.

About three years ago, Channel 5 ABC TV, invited the
entire membership of the Council to review a three-
part series on Sex Education in local schools to determine the acceptability of such a program on commercial television and our preference as to hours to be
shown. They followed our suggestions and the series
was successfully presented.

This year our president was invited along with newspaper critics and representatives of the same station
to view a controversial movie "The Damned" due to
the public furor regarding it.

One of our members, Mr. J. Jerome Lackamp,
testified before the FCC on behalf of the public regarding station license renewals this month, representing our Council and two other organizations.

Radio and TV stations respond to our monthly bulletins
and Selective Dialing brochure if our comments affect
them negatively. So they do pay attention to us!

Finally, we feel that we represent a cross-section of
Greater Cleveland, not merely upper middle-class.
Representatives range from inner city schools, public
and parochial, to members of DAR groups. Yes, the
majority are women who actively participate in this
work.[13]

In terms of an objective evaluation of the effectiveness of the
council, such an assessment could probably best be made by Cleveland
area broadcasters, and by other media concerned with broadcasting,
such as newspaper broadcast critics and columnists.

A vice president and general manager of a network television affiliate in Cleveland stated in a letter to the council,

> We hope that, in some measure, our support of your worthwhile endeavor helped accomplish your goals. For, in some part, your goals are our goals. . . . We're committed to serving the needs and interests of the people in our community and it is through your suggestions, advice, and counsel that we can continually enhance our service in all areas. . . . I can assure you that we look forward toward a continuing and productive association. [14]

The same station shows on the air the council's seal as a public service, and the slides of the seal were produced free of charge by another Cleveland television station.

Ted Baze, program director of WUAB-TV, Channel 43, Cleveland, Ohio, wrote,

> We do have a certain amount of respect for the Council as I am sure do most of the other broadcasters in the area. Their intentions are good and, to my knowledge, they have never used their organization to apply any pressure tactics on the broadcasting industry. They seriously attempt to make friends with the broadcaster and to educate themselves on the problems of the industry. I regularly attend their meetings and seriously consider the ideas they present that pertain to programming as well as community interests and needs.

> Their publication called <u>Selective Dialing</u> is probably one of their greater weaknesses. It contains some inaccuracies and I am sure is based, to a degree, on the information provided by the stations themselves. While they recommend and encourage certain types of programs, generally the "quality" or educational type, a survey indicated that their viewing habits almost exactly paralleled those of the general public as reported by the rating services. In fact, one of our most loyal wrestling fans is executive vice-president of the organization.

> The Council is, I am sure, of some benefit to the local broadcasting community and I am also sure that any community would benefit by having such an organization

especially if their aim was toward the direction of
educating themselves about broadcasting as does
our local group. [15]

Donald L. Perris, general manager of WEWS-TV, wrote,

In my opinion the Council is regarded as a constructive
and well-informed group by Cleveland broadcasters. It
is very warmly regarded by us at WEWS. The Council
is definitely respected. The reasons for this respect
are that it has been knowledgeable in its field, with
members looking at programs for themselves and
drawing their own conclusions. This independence of
thought, combined with the fact the group has often
found things to praise rather than just constantly con-
demning, has made us respect its attitudes.

We feel the Council is beneficial and do consult them,
and their attitudes do play a part in our programming
decisions. Selective Dialing is worthwhile, in my
opinion. [16]

Joe Varholy, program manager at WKYC-TV, an NBC affiliate,
wrote,

The Cleveland Council has an excellent working relationship with WKYC. We are pleased that they take the time
to get involved in various projects for the betterment of
the community. We respect the Council and what it's attempting to achieve and we assume the other stations
feel the same way. We believe that their membership
is generally representative of the Cleveland television
audience, but might question their minority representation.

As I indicated, we have a good relationship with the
Council and that includes providing them with speakers
for their events and conducting seminars in our studios
for their membership. We feel that Selective Dialing
is a meaningful publication and would hope that its
distribution is adequate.

In closing, I would suggest that the Council's membership take a more active part in its affairs. I have heard

from members holding official positions with the
organization that the membership is apathetic and
not responsive to the goals of the organization. [17]

Both broadcast columnists in the two Cleveland metropolitan
daily newspapers have written articles on the council and its activities.
Cleveland Press columnist Bill Barrett discussed the council's annual
evaluation of local stations. He complimented the council members:
"They are thoroughly knowledgeable about the field of broadcasting,
these women, and they and the groups they represent hold enormous
clout. I salute them." [18]

THE CLEVELAND COUNCIL: SUMMARY

The Greater Cleveland Radio and Television Council appears
to be a well-organized group. That its membership represents over
60 civic and cultural organizations seems to speak well for the council's ability to attract members. Varholy raised some interesting
questions when he said he might question the council's minority representation. This statement probably could be supported by Lipset's
sociological observation cited in Chapter 2, which noted that usually
only certain types of persons tend to participate politically and
civically. Varholy, the only Cleveland broadcaster who offered possible critical views of the council, also suggested the group's membership tended to be apathetic and "not responsive."

His suggestion indicates another possible limitation from his
perspective. The council may serve more as a "social" or expressive
association than as an instrumental (action-oriented) organization.
Possibly it has fulfilled both functions for such members.

A third possible limitation could be that since most of the
council members are women, it might be concerned primarily with
programming for women and children, such as programs on child-
raising, cooking, home decorating, and so on.

These limitations—if they could be termed limitations—could
be regarded also as strengths. If the council attracted members for
social purposes, possibly the members could later turn more of
their attention to instrumental purposes. Also, that the majority of
the members are women does not necessarily restrict their interests
to "programming for women," nor does it mean that such interests
are not productive. Female broadcast audiences might provide a
more consistent audience and larger daytime audience than a male
audience.

The council's other strength appears to be perpetuating itself and attracting new members. That the group is more than 30 years old speaks well for its organizational ability. In general, having the support and respect of local stations and having three decades of experience to draw on, seems to indicate that the Greater Cleveland Radio and Television Council well could be a model for other cities to consider, as the FCC and Siepmann pointed out more than 25 years ago.

Other community councils mentioned in the literature of broadcasting, which apparently have been similar in scope and operation to the Cleveland group, were the Wisconsin Association for Better Radio and Television in Madison, the Massachusetts Association for Better Radio and Television in Boston, and the Illinois Council on Motion Pictures, Radio-Television, and Publications in Chicago.[19] Preliminary investigation revealed them to have the same general nature as the Cleveland council.

ACTION FOR CHILDREN'S TELEVISION

If the Greater Cleveland Radio and Television Council could be described as a community-based, expressive-instrumental association that has maintained "congenial" relations with stations, Action for Children's Television could be cited as an instrumental citizens' group not concerned with a specific community and apparently not interested in maintaining friendly relations with broadcasters.

Action for Children's Television (ACT) has been selected as an example of a citizens' group concerned with broadcasting primarily at the national level. It is a women's group organized in 1968 at Newtonville, Massachusetts, when a group of mothers began discussing television programs for children. The group began to grow and its major emphasis shifted to network television for youngsters. The Wall Street Journal reported in 1970 that ACT had 500 members in 28 states.[20] TV Guide stated earlier that year that ACT claimed a membership of nearly 1,000 members in 18 states.[21] Evelyn Sarson, ACT executive director, wrote,

> Our total membership is difficult to estimate. We have over a thousand people across the country who have sent dues and therefore joined financially so that we consider them a paying member. We have some 5,000 people we call supporters since they are either actively working for us, or have written indicating support, but haven't paid

up. And then we consider our <u>constituency</u> the over
100,000 individuals and groups, which represent
millions of people, who wrote to the FCC in its
recent inquiry into children's television in support
of ACT.[22]

According to one of ACT's newsletters, the group

> began when a group of parents, educators and others
> concerned with children tried to find out how to raise
> the quality of children's TV programs. ACT formulated
> guidelines to set basic ground rules for children's TV
> that would: Protect children from the particularly crude
> and cynical pressure tactics which are the special char-
> acteristics of commercials on children's shows; sub-
> stitute a new system of financing support for children's
> programs by commercial underwriting and public service
> fundings; create a climate for quality programming in
> which children are regarded as a special audience, and
> programming in which producers and performers are
> relieved from commercial pressures.[23]

ACT is a nonprofit organization with individual membership
dues beginning at $5.00. A benefactor is a person who contributes
a membership fee of $500. ACT has employed an advisory board
composed of Hyman H. Goldin, associate professor of communications
at Boston University School of Public Communication; FCC consultant
John Condry, professor of psychology, Cornell University; Richard
Galdston, chief, psychiatric consultation service, Children's Hospital,
Boston, Massachusetts; Milton Akers, director, National Association
for Education of Young Children, Washington D.C.; and Richard Lewis,
poet, editor, and director of the Touchstone Center for Children,
New York, New York.[24] In 1972, ACT received a $164,500 grant
from the John and Mary Markle Foundation.[25] In May, 1974, ACT
received a grant of $300,000 from the Ford Foundation and the Markle
Foundation providing funding for another two years.
      In October 1970, ACT, supported by a grant from the Ford
Foundation, held a National Symposium on Children and Television
at Newtonville, Massachusetts. The papers presented at the symposium have been published in paperback by Avon Books, entitled
<u>Action for Children's Television</u>.[26] The event was attended by a
number of educators, attorneys, physicians, congressmen, and
broadcasters. A second symposium co-hosted by the American
Academy of Pediatrics was held in 1971. A third was conducted in
October 1972.[27]

ACT makes available to various groups a 16-mm 15-minute color film, "But First, This Message." The unique film uses clips from TV programs, statements from professional educators, and comments from children. The association also provides a free resource list of studies of broadcasting, legal documents with the FCC and the Federal Trade Commission (FTC), and its newsletter. [28]

The citizens' group has members and "contacts" in a total of 67 communities representing nearly every state. ACT contacts "often participate in ACT projects that require the monitoring of children's television; they distribute ACT materials locally, stimulate interest in children's broadcasting, and encourage membership. There is also an ACT contact and chapter in Macleod, Victoria, Australia. [29]

ACT received an award for the group's "highly effective contributions to the welfare of the community by their dedicated efforts for the improvement of the quality and quantity of children's programs," by the Board of Supervisors of the City and County of San Francisco in 1972. [30]

In contrast with the Cleveland council, which tends to limit its activity to evaluating local stations, ACT takes a more active stance and engages in a number of action-oriented activities. These include a "letter write-in" demonstration at which balloons were handed out in April 1970 at New York City's Central Park urging people to write the FCC to support ACT's position. [31] The organization also sponsored two studies to support its petition to the FCC requesting the commission (1) to eliminate television commercials on children's programs and (2) to set a minimum of 14 hours per week for noncommercial children's programs. The statistical study was directed by Ralph Jennings (now with the United Church of Christ's Communication Section), who selected representative samples of stations in the top 50 U.S. television markets. The second study involved a pilot study by Daniel Yankelovich, Incorporated, an attitudinal research firm, which examined "mothers' attitudes toward children's television programs and commercials." [32]

Also, four ACT committee members confered with chief executives of CBS Television Network and discussed "excessive commercialism, the low caliber of children's programming in general, the lack of a specific children's television executive at CBS, and the need for a national understanding that would grant children's TV the status of public service programming and recognize children as a special audience and not just as miniature consumers." [33]

In 1972 ACT joined several other citizens' groups in filing a petition to deny the license renewal application for continuing use of channel 11 in Los Angeles, California, owned by Metromedia. Other groups participating were the National Association for Better Broadcasting, the Mexican American Political Association, and the Fair Housing Council of San Fernando Valley. The petition stated in part that the television station broadcast" . . . a vast quantity of old, outworn and violence-ridden programs for children which are, in part, harmful to the mental and physical welfare of child audiences."[34]

Perhaps ACT's most significant accomplishments include the filing of petitions with both the FCC and FTC regarding television commercials designed for children. With the legal assistance of another citizens' group, Citizens Communication Center, in early 1970 ACT filed its formal petition with the FCC "seeking a total ban on commercials during children's TV shows."[35] And in February 1970, the FCC published ACT's guidelines for children's television in the form of a public notice. The guidelines stated (1) that there be a minimum of 14 hours programming for children of different ages each week as a public service, (2) that there be no commercials on children's programs, and (3) that hosts on children's programs do no selling.[36]

The publishing of ACT's guidelines as a public notice and rule making inquiry meant that the commission was inviting comments from both the public and the broadcast industry regarding the proposals. According to Parade, ACT members were "astounded at the support their activities have attracted throughout the country." When ACT filed its petition, "more than 100,000 letters poured into the FCC offices in favor of their position."[37] But beyond publishing the guidelines, the FCC has not acted.

The broadcasting industry, however, did act. TV Guide reported, "The very fact that FCC would consider such directives at once heartened parent-educator forces and struck fear in the power centers in broadcasting." ABC network was reported to have said ACT's proposals are in "direct and irreconcilable conflict with the Commission's proper and historical role."[38] ABC, however, subsequently reduced the number of commercials that the network carried for children. CBS termed ACT's proposals "self-defeating." And Palmer Broadcasting Group, which has stations in Iowa and Florida, said the proposal was "unconstitutional." Kern Broadcasting Company said commercials benefited children in that "improved vocabularies, increased knowledge and expanded experiences may result from children's commercials."[39]

Another group—the National Confectioners Association—responded, "This is a scheme to 'kill the goose which lays the golden eggs'—if the goose is sick, let the broadcasters, consumers and sponsors, not the FCC, 'improve its health.' " And the American Association of Advertising Agencies said the idea was "ill-advised" because the proposal, if adopted, would deprive the broadcaster of income he needs to "raise his program standards."[40] Saturday Review broadcast critic Shayon described ACT's proposal to the FCC as a "very hot brick that the Commission will have to come to terms with sooner or later."[41]

In its petition, ACT's attorneys asked the FCC to make substantial time available by the broadcasters for the presentation on the air of Federal Trade Commission (FTC) notices on deceptive advertising of children's toys. ACT's lawyers argued that under the fairness doctrine broadcasters were required to grant free air time to warn parents of allegedly deceptive advertising. ACT also offered to supply 123 television stations in the top 25 markets with announcements warning parents about "interdicted ads." None of the stations elected to use them.[42]

In November 1971, ACT filed another petition with the FTC seeking to bar all advertising of vitamins and other drugs on children's programs and on family shows. It contended that advertising those types of products are unfair and misleading. The petition stated,

> . . . . In the next decade we may see advertising
> directed to children used to promote an even wider
> and less child-oriented range of products as a growing
> number of advertisers realize that you can sell anything
> to a child through television.[43]

In testimony before the FTC, Evelyn Sarson, ACT's executive director, said ACT was "unhappy and disappointed over a lack of responsibility shown in this area by the networks."[44]

In asking for a ban on such commercials, ACT policy was based on the premise that "children were not equipped to make an adult judgment or decision on advertising as to apparent misleading or deceptive approaches" and that children lack the maturity or experience to analyze what an ACT spokesman termed "normal puffery claims of commercials."[45]

In addition to filing petitions, ACT engaged in other activities such as appearing before the Senate committee meetings. In fall 1969, Lillian Ambrosino and Peggy Charren testified before Senator John Pastore's committee hearings on the appointment of Burch and Wells to the FCC. At the hearings, Ambrosino stated,

> We are asking that children's television be seen as
> a public service, whose mandate is to be as non-com-
> mercial as possible. . . . we are not asking broad-
> casters to become substitute parents. Television
> should be a joint responsibility of both parents and
> broadcasters. Our job as parents is to supervise
> our children's viewing of television programs de-
> signed for adults. We should not have to look over
> their shoulders when they are watching children's
> programs.[46]

As noted earlier, neither the FCC nor the FTC has taken final action regarding regulation based on ACT's proposals. Concerning the possibility of such regulations, TV Guide stated, "The likelihood of the FCC actually implementing rules growing out of ACT's proposals seems quite remote. It would go beyond any regulations the FCC has yet ventured."[47]

ACT'S TENTATIVE CONCLUSIONS

In response to a 60-second spot announcement that the Television Information Office of the NAB prepared to "prove to the public that children's television on commercial stations was informative and enlightening," ACT filed a petition with the FCC for a decision under the fairness doctrine asking that "stations airing the spot be required to air opposing opinions on this issue . . . to let the public know that some people think that much of TV is over-commercial, exploitive, violent."[48]

In addition to its frequent criticism of commercial broadcasting, ACT bestowed awards to commercial and noncommercial stations for "significant steps towards upgrading children's television, and for eliminating commercialism on children's programs." Examples of such awards would include ACT Rewards Achievements to (1) Post-Newsweek television stations in Washington, D.C., and in Florida for "seeking out quality programs for children; for clustering commercials on such programs; (2) to Robert Keeshan for sixteen years of devotion to creative television for preschool children on "Captain Kangaroo;" and (3) to "The Kids Thing," WHDH-TV, Boston, for providing five special half-hour programs for children during a school vacation week without commercials.[49]

Moreover, United Press International broadcast editor, Rick DuBrow, wrote,

> Public criticism of children's television programs is forcing the networks to develop new serious concepts for youngsters. . . .
>
> The idea of after-school programming by the commercial networks seems so obvious and needed that one wouldn't think outside criticism and pressure would be required to get it on. But in fact such outside heat is precisely what is often needed to get the networks to put on the kinds of broadcasts that may not hold the promise of overpowering ratings and great financial rewards.[50]

DuBrow attributes not only outside criticism but also the influence of noncommercial children's programs such as "Sesame Street" in helping prompt the networks to alter their programs for children.

Possibly in response to ACT's activities, ABC announced in December 1971 that it would reduce by one-third the number of commercials on children's television programs. James B. Duffy, ABC president, said such changes were due and indicated that if the industry did not adopt such changes, the FTC or "another Federal agency might well crack down on broadcasters."[51]

And in January 1972 the Code Authority of the NAB said it had reduced by four minutes the 16 minutes of advertising per hour on children's weekend programs and the number of interruptions such as billboards, commercials, promotional announcements, and credits in excess of 30 seconds would be cut in half. The changes and reductions became effective in January 1973.[52] And, as mentioned earlier, in June 1974 the NAB again decided to reduce the number of commercials on children's weekend television programs. The Television Code of the NAB defines children's weekend programming time as the following:

> That contiguous period of time between the hours of 7:00 a.m. and 2:00 p.m. on Saturday and Sunday. In programming designed primarily for children within this time period, non-program material shall not exceed 12 minutes in any 60-minute period.[53]

In one of its newsletters, ACT responded,

> While ACT applauds this move as a change in the right direction, it notes sadly: 1) the change will not begin until January, 1973, after the hard sell of the Christmas season of 1972; 2) the change applies only to Saturday and Sunday, and ignores the daytime hours of Monday through Friday, five-sevenths of the week; 3) there is no suggestion that this is the beginning of a series of changes to bring ads on children's programs to a level below that on adult programs, or to remove them altogether.

The ACT article added that 40 percent of television stations do not even subscribe to the NAB Code and "the subscribers who violate the present code are rarely disciplined."[54]

Regarding the group's major activities, and the extent to which its members have influenced broadcasters, Sarson stated,

> There is no count of how many members have met with local stations—several certainly have. I think our major effect has been in "consciousness raising" about children's

television, and in showing many professionals who deal
with children that television is now a major factor in a
child's growing up. [55]

In 1972, ACT was "writing to the people who wrote to the FCC and
asking them to join ACT and hope eventually to have a membership
of 100,000—or even more."[56] Sarson observed in 1972,

> We're not against advertising as such. . . . we're
> not a censorship group or a watch-and-ward society.
> But we think advertising of specific children's pro-
> ducts such as toys or cereals, should be directed
> at the parents. They are the true consumers—the
> ones who have to pay. Advertising on children's
> programs should be purely institutional.[57]

Former ACT president Charren added,

> We don't know how far we're going to get. . . . But
> we're making noise. Maybe the most important thing
> we've done has been to just get people to look at what
> the television broadcasters are showing to their child-
> ren. That ought to be enough to make them want to do
> something about it.[58]

TV Guide credited the organization by stating,

> It was ACT, as much as any other organization in
> the U.S., that launched all the sound and fury against
> violence in children's programming— alerting the
> the entire Nation to the fact that while it lay abed
> of a Saturday morning, cartoon heroes were zapping
> cartoon villains and monsters with sinister regularity.[59]

In discussing violence on television, Reader's Digest also credited
ACT with helping improve programming for children, for reducing
the number of commercials on children's programs, and for increasing national awareness in that area in broadcasting.[60]

Given the extent of public support that ACT has received and
given its ability to attract financial support from two large foundations, ACT's growth since its inception in 1968 seems remarkable.
That it has been able to attract national attention and persuade the
FCC to issue a "Notice of Inquiry Proposal" attests to its organizational and legal strengths. As an instrumental goal-oriented citizens'
group, ACT has accomplished much in its brief existence.

OTHER NATIONAL CITIZENS' GROUPS

There are several other contemporary citizens' groups concerned with broadcasting that have been similar to ACT in that they were not community-oriented; they seek a national base. They also have monitored programs and evaluated programs, sending their opinions by mail to both broadcasters (networks and local stations) and to advertisers as well as the FCC. Such groups were different from ACT in that ACT's primary goal was the improvement of television for children. The other groups, while being interested in broadcasting for children, have not confined their activities to that end and have been interested in other aspects of broadcasting.

Such groups include the American Council for Better Broadcasts; the National Association for Better Broadcasting; the United Church of Christ; the National Citizens Committee for Broadcasting. There also have been general organizations, such as the National Organization for Women and the General Federation of Women's Clubs, which have had local chapters interested in improving broadcasting.

Preliminary investigation indicates that although each of these groups tends to operate differently and at its own level, each has interests similar to those of ACT.

CITIZENS COMMUNICATIONS CENTER

The third citizens' group to be used as a case study will be that of a specialized citizens' organization: the Citizens Communications Center (CCC). This organization has been selected because of the nature of its operation. It has been a type of support group offering legal and procedural expertise to the public and to other citizens' organizations concerned with broadcasting. Since it does not seek a large lay membership, it couldn't be classified as an expressive association. Conceivably it could be termed as a small instrumental group.

CCC was formed in mid-August 1969 in Washington, D. C., with assistance from the RFK Memorial.[61] In early 1972, the center received a $400,000 grant from the Ford Foundation. The center previously had been receiving support from a "number of smaller foundations, including the Rockefeller Brothers Fund, the Midas International Foundation, and the Stern Family Fund." The Ford grant is used to pay the salaries of the executive director, Frank W. Lloyd, the center's three attorneys, and the office and administrative expenses, as well as litigation costs for two years. The

grant also will support the center's information program. CCC has
a 10-man board of directors headed by Sidney Sachs, a former president of the Washington, D. C. Bar Association.[62] Also on the board is
Henry Geller, former general counsel to the FCC. Its current director
joined the center in 1973 and was former general counsel of the National Public Affairs Center for Television. According to CCC's
statement of purpose,

> The broadcast industry often has not understood—or has
> chosen to ignore—the programming tastes and require-
> ments of broad portions of the viewing public. There
> has existed no formal means for public spirited citizens
> to directly influence what is presented over the airwaves.
> The problem has been particularly acute for minority
> groups—whether they be racial, ethnic, political or
> economic—who are especially dependent on the airwaves
> for developing a dialogue with, and present[ing] their view-
> points to, the society at large.[63]

Albert Kramer, former executive director and founder of the
Center, noted that a number of citizens' groups have come into existence to exercise the right to participate before the FCC as parties
in cases affecting their interests.

> Nineteen local groups protested the alleged rightwing
> programming of a station in Pennsylvania. Young
> Blacks objected to the lack of relevant community
> orientation in the programming of stations in St. Louis
> and Dayton. Good music groups have fought the loss
> of classical music in Chicago, Seattle, and Atlanta.
> A union complained that it could not get its messages
> on stations in Ohio. A young New York lawyer obtained,
> and then enforced a FCC ruling requiring the broadcasting
> of information regarding the health hazards of smoking.
> Local groups have, or are, attempting to regain local
> ownerships and control of large corporate television
> stations in New York, Los Angeles, and Boston. A
> church has urged the FCC to issue equal employment
> opportunity regulations.
>
> This scattered and accelerating activity has created
> a need for coordination and professional service
> center in Washington. There is, at the present time,
> no single professional resource to which these citizens
> can turn. The organizations that do exist are staffed

principally with relatively unsophisticated lay volunteers. The FCC is woefully understaffed, and to some extent prohibited as a matter of propriety from providing meaningful legal assistance to those who may become parties before it. Most local lawyers outside the Washington-based "Federal Communications Bar Association" are simply at a total loss in dealing with the unfamiliar intricacies of FCC procedures. The Center will attempt to fill this gap by performing, without charge for its services, a number of functions. [64]

CCC's activities tend to fall into three categories: (1) opening the federal regulatory process to adversary procedures and participation by citizens: (2) aiding citizens and groups with resources or technical skills in participating in the regulatory and decision-making process and obtaining media access; and (3) informing citizens' and community groups of their rights to participate in those processes, to have access to the broadcast media, and educate and train advocates to assert these rights. [65]

Following were some of its specific functions: preparation and distribution of basic factual manuals on citizens' rights to access to the media and on FCC procedures; provide complainants with rudimentary legal and strategic advice and counsel; refer complainants to lawyers or to other professional services; provide research and other services for citizens' groups at the FCC; offer coordinating functions such as referrals and conferences and training institutes; and serve as an information center to provide local groups with information about legislative, judicial, and administrative proceedings that may affect broadcasting. [66] Among its accomplished activities the center has

1. provided research and legal counsel for citizens' groups challenging KRON-TV in San Francisco, WMAL-TV in Washington, D.C., WSNT-AM in Sandersville, Georgia, and stations in Mobile, Alabama;

2. represented groups, such as the Business Executive Move for Vietnam Peace (BEM) and the Quaker Church in their attempts to establish first amendment rights of "free access" to television stations for broadcasting advertisements opposing the Vietnam War and the draft;

3. responded to requests for nonpartisan and informational research of Pastore's bill to amend the Communications Act;

4. helped organize and direct a "Nader's Raiders" investigation of the FCC;

5. compiled an equal employment opportunity handbook for minority groups in broadcasting; and

6. compiled a handbook on citizens' access to the FCC.[67]

Perhaps CCC's most significant achievements have included the center's intervention in the transaction involving McGraw-Hill, Incorporated, and Time, Incorporated, broadcast stations. CCC, representing a coalition of eight Mexican-American and one black group, was able to prevent McGraw-Hill's acquisition of five stations. The McGraw-Hill firm acquired four stations from Time-Life Broadcast, Incorporated. The station WOOD-TV, Grand Rapids, Michigan, was omitted from the transaction. CCC stated in its petition to the FCC that the commission should have enforced its top 50 market policy to promote diversification of ownership of television stations. CCC also was able to persuade McGraw-Hill to make "extensive agreements to citizens' groups" including commitments in programming, use of citizen-advisory councils, employment, training programs and public access to the stations' facilities.[68]

Kramer said McGraw-Hill's decision to acquire only four of the five stations was "the private enforcement of a public law." The firm's decision was "part of the price McGraw-Hill was required to pay" to persuade the groups to withdraw the suits filed in the United States Court of Appeals to overturn the FCC's approval of the transaction. The appeals were dismissed as soon as the settlement was signed.[69]

In another transaction described in Chapter 3 involving the transfer of station ownership from Triangle Publications, Incorporated, to Capital Cities Broadcasting Company, CCC obtained "numerous concessions" including a commitment by the stations to spend $1 million on minority-interest programming. The concession was made in return for the withdrawal of protests against Capital Cities' proposed acquisition of Triangle stations. Citizens' groups existed in each of the cities where Capital Cities bought stations: New Haven, Connecticut, Philadelphia, Pennsylvania, and Fresno, California. The groups were assured they would be consulted in the production of $1 million worth of local programming in the next three years.[70]

Broadcasting described CCC's intervention in the BEM case, "which drastically widened the concept of 'access to the air' and its representation of minority groups" in the Capital Cities transaction, as a "significant" victory.[71]

The center's other activities included requesting the FCC to adopt rules allowing public inspection of financial reports of broadcast licensees. The proposal asked for a listing of expenditures on specific types of programming—news, public affairs, and total local programming. The proposal stated, "A station's performance at renewal time should be measured in substantial part by the extent to which it 're-invests' its profits and resources in locally-oriented programming." CCC was joined in this request by the Stern Community Law Firm, another private legal resource center, and the National Citizens Committee for Broadcasting.[72]

TV Guide described Kramer as the "busiest lawyer" in the legal assistance area.

> He has about 20 petitions pending at any one time, and helps other groups. He worries about some of the people who come to him: "One of the problems about opening up a regulatory process to democratization," he says, "is that you can get in unseemly groups." But a strong belief in a basic cause can override even Kramer's scruples about the clients he wants to represent. His cause is simply stated: "To get these groups access in the decision-making process on the programming that people can see."[73]

When Kramer announced that he was leaving CCC in July 1973, Broadcasting Magazine stated,

> . . . Mr. Kramer has accomplished what observers generally regard as a substantial record with the fragile tool (of the law used by citizens groups). The petitions to deny license renewals that Citizens (Communications Center) has filed against scores of stations over the years have helped sensitize broadcasters to the needs and demands of groups in their communities, even if few stations have actually lost licenses. Furthermore, Citizens has helped negotiate agreements under which stations, in return for the withdrawal of a petition to deny, have promised to pursue the kind of employment and programming practices local citizens regard as being in the public interest.[74]

Kramer, according to the trade journal, said his experiences as a public interest attorney in broadcasting taught him that citizens' groups can employ the law as their "fragile tool" in dealing with stations. He added that broadcasters "have overwhelming resources" in terms of money, legal help, and the advantage of close relationships with the FCC.

His successor, Frank Lloyd, was on the staff of the Washington, D.C., law firm of Wilmer, Cutler & Pickering before he joined the National Public Affairs Center for Television (NPACT). He also had been general counsel at the Office of Economic Opportunity for one year.[75]

To place CCC within some form of political framework, it will be helpful to return to several points mentioned in the first chapter, which described the increased interest in consumerism and its application to broadcasting.

That chapter noted some of the historic shortcomings of the FCC and how the commission over the years tended to ignore or discourage public participation. Also noted was the degree to which broadcasters, as businessmen, usually seek their own self interests. CCC was formed to help offset those aspects in broadcast matters and to help members of the public participate in the democratic process.

In a sense, CCC could be described as an issue-oriented private organization, designed to facilitate public representation involving the allocation and use of a public resource. It could be also described as a public interest law firm concerned with broadcasting and the public.

Indeed, one of the center's goals is the establishment of a type of "Nader's Raiders" team to investigate the FCC. In the proposed study, a group of young, enthusiastic, and capable persons would conduct an in-depth study of that government agency.

As described in Chapter 1, Kramer said the beneficial part of consumerism in broadcasting is that people can become involved in the decision-making process. "People want back more control over their lives."

It would be difficult to assess the center's record in terms of "success" or "failure" for several reasons. CCC has been involved both directly and indirectly, as well as formally and informally, in a number of legal and nonlegal actions against broadcasters and the FCC. As a direct participant, CCC has signed formal and legal petitions in matters that may take years to settle through the courts. And some issues may be settled out of court.

On an informal and indirect basis, the center has aided citizens' groups by offering free legal counsel and helping gather data and information for various groups to assist in their dealings with both the FCC and broadcast stations. In these instances, the degree to which CCC has provided assistance has not been made public; nor is there any measurable means of determining the amount of assistance provided.

In summary, CCC has helped various groups through different means and has initiated some public interest causes in broadcast matters. That the Ford Foundation and other institutions have provided financial support to the center attests in some measure to its success. Such institutions would not, ordinarily, provide donations to a resource center that was not operating efficiently or without some degree of success. The actual existence of CCC might serve as a catalyst or as an encouragement to other citizens' groups, which might not organize themselves unless they believe they have access to legal and procedural advice. This could be described as a form of "intangible" success. That <u>Broadcasting</u> described CCC's influence in the BEM case and in the Capital Cities transaction as "significant victories" indicates how the broadcast industry apparently perceives the center's activities.

It would seem safe to conclude that CCC probably will continue to exist and participate in broadcast matters—if its sources of funds are not terminated. That is its greatest potential weakness, a reliance on foundations for financial support. Another possible weakness is its small size. That its activities are run by a miniscule staff could weaken its operating efficiency. Yet smallness can be strength at times, since the center could be flexible and unencumbered.

Unless the interest in consumerism in broadcasting is diminished, CCC and the other public interest resource centers probably will continue their activities.

OTHER SUPPORT GROUPS

The CCC has been joined in a number of actions by other private groups similar in nature to it. The group that most frequently associates with the CCC is the Stern Community Law Firm, directed by Tracy Westen, once an aide to former Commissioner Johnson. The Stern Firm is supported by the Philip M. Stern Family Fund. There is also the Stern Concern, another private group concerned with broadcasting, based in Los Angeles.[76]

Another private group active in providing legal and procedural information to citizens' groups is the Communications Office of the United Church of Christ. Probably one of the earliest resource organizations, the United Church of Christ was instrumental in the landmark WLBT-TV case mentioned earlier. The church's activities have been directed by Everett Parker, who said the church has helped "hundreds or organizations" across the nation. His office has received three grants from the Ford Foundation for a total of $530,000.[77]

There have been several other recent organizations formed to provide legal advice or assistance to citizens' groups. The Monroe County Legal Assistance Corporation was listed with CCC on petitions opposing license renewal applications of 14 stations in Monroe County, New York. Other such groups include Lawyers for the Center of Law and Social Policy, the Institute for Public Interest Representatives (INSPIRE) at Georgetown University Law Center, in Washington, D.C., the Women's Legal Defense Fund, and the Legal Aid Society of Albany, New York.[78]

TENTATIVE CONCLUSIONS

It would appear that all the brief case studies described in this chapter, the Greater Cleveland Radio and Television Council, Action for Children's Television, and Citizens Communications Center, have been effective—to a limited extent. The only group that seems to have earned the respect of broadcasters has been the Cleveland council, probably because it has sought to work <u>with,</u> and not <u>against,</u> broadcast stations. Yet evidence indicates that ACT and CCC apparently have been instrumental in effectuating change that probably would not have occurred if these groups had not acted.

That these two organizations and other citizens' bodies have been able to influence decisions indicates two things. First, that the goals of ACT and CCC are attainable; and these groups had the tenacity, the finances, the manpower, and the expertise to achieve them. Second, that perhaps "the system" of broadcasting in this country—including the FCC and the 1934 Communications Act—is less than perfect and that changes are in order. This raises still a larger question. Why were such changes not brought about earlier, and how many aspects of broadcasting need to be or will be changed in the future. It hardly seems likely that the widespread interest in consumerism will lessen. Obviously, ACT and CCC were created to fill a need at a period when consumers were responsive to such organizations. Even if private foundations were to terminate their financial support of those two organizations, it seems possible that ACT and CCC could survive drawing support from individual membership fees or possibly charging for services.

Former FCC Commissioner Johnson observed, "We are witnessing on all sides today a revolution of 'participatory democracy.' " Possibly this nation is, and the emergence of citizens' groups is one manifestation of this change. It would be easy to conclude that citizens' organizations are panaceas to the abuses and problems of commercial broadcasting. But, as noted in Chapters 1 and 2, they have had limitations. Johnson stated that citizens' groups and audience members

> . . . . are not generally too helpful when it comes to
> suggesting new program ideas. What many organizations
> <u>think</u> would be a good program often turns out to be a dud.
> When offered free air-time, many organizations do not
> take it, or do not follow through for a sustained period.[79]

But he added that station managers have not been blameless either.

NOTES

1. "The Revolt Against Radio," Fortune 35, No. 3 (March 1947): 175.

2. Charles Siepmann, Radio, Televison and Society (New York: Oxford University Press, 1960), p. 77.

3. Broadcasting Yearbook 1973 (Washington, D. C.: Broadcasting Publications, Inc., 1973), pp. A41-42 and p. B153.

4. Letter from Mrs. A. J. Matkovick, June 29, 1971.

5. Ibid.

6. Ibid.

7. Llewellyn White, American Radio: A Report on the Broadcast Industry in the United States from the Commission on Freedom of the Press (Chicago: University of Chicago Press, 1947), p. 114.

8. Radio-Television Council of Greater Cleveland, Regulations of the Radio-Television Council of Greater Cleveland, (Cleveland: Radio-Television Council of Greater Cleveland, 1971), p. 7.

9. Radio-Television Council of Greater Cleveland, Standing Rules of the Greater Cleveland Radio and Television Council, (Cleveland: Radio-Television Council of Greater Cleveland, 1971).

10. Ibid.

11. Cleveland Press, February 17, 1972.

12. Cleveland Press, May 4, 1972.

13. Letter from Evelyn Slough, June 13, 1972.

14. Letter from Neal A. Van Ells, vice president and general manager, WKYC-TV, Cleveland, Ohio, to Mrs. R. Bartunek, president of Greater Cleveland Radio and Television Council, March 27, 1972.

15. Letter from Ted Baze, June 22, 1972.

16. Letter from Donald L. Perris, June 27, 1972.

17. Letter from Joe Varholy, June 28, 1972.

18. Cleveland Press, May 4, 1972.

19. O. Joe Olson, ed., Education On The Air (Columbus: Ohio State University Press, 1953), pp. 229-41.

20. Wall Street Journal, October 22, 1970.

21. "Boston Tea Party-1970," TV Guide, July 4, 1970, p. 14.

22. Letter from Evelyn Sarson, June 7, 1972.

23. ACT Newsletter 1, No. 3 (summer 1970).

24. Ibid.

25. "Markle Grants for Studies Seek Quality in Journalism," Editor & Publisher, April 2, 1972, p. 46.

26. Evelyn Sarson, ed., Action for Children's Television (New York: Avon Books, 1971), p. 3.

27. ACT Newsletter 3, No. 1 (spring/summer 1972), p. 2.

28. Ibid., p. 8.

29. ACT Newsletter 3 (winter 1973); 4, No. 2 (winter 1974); 4, No. 1 (spring/summer 1974).

30. ACT Newsletter (spring/summer 1972), op. cit., p. 5.

31. ACT Newsletter (summer 1970), op. cit., p. 2.

32. Ibid.

33. ACT Newsletter 1, No. 2 (January/February 1970).

34. ACT Newsletter (spring/summer 1972), op. cit., p. 2.

35. ACT Newsletter (summer 1970), op. cit.

36. Ibid., p. 2.

37. "Your Kids Need Better TV - You Can Help," Parade, January 30, 1972, p. 20.

38. TV Guide, July 4, 1970, op. cit.

39. Ibid.

40. Ibid.

41. Robert Lewis Shayon, "Caveat Pre-Emptor," Saturday Review, January 9, 1971, p. 37.

42. Ibid.

43. "ACT Goes Back to The FCC," Broadcasting, December 20, 1971, p. 46.

44. Ibid., p. 45.

46. ACT Newsletter (January-February 1970), op. cit.

47. TV Guide, July 4, 1970, op. cit., p. 16.

48. ACT Newsletter (spring/summer 1972), op. cit., p. 5.

49. Ibid., p. 3.

50. Oregon Journal, May 25, 1972.

51. Parade, January 30, 1972, op. cit.

52. The Code Authority of the National Association of Broadcasters, Code News (New York: National Association of Broadcasters, 1972) 4, No. 11 (February, 1972).

53. National Association of Broadcasters, The Television Code (New York: National Association of Broadcasters, 1972), p. 19.

54. ACT Newsletter (spring/summer 1972), op. cit., p. 4.

55. Sarson letter, op. cit.

56. Parade, January 30, 1972, op. cit.

57. Ibid.

58. Ibid.

59. "The Children's Crusade That Failed," TV Guide 21, No. 14 (April 7, 1973): 7.

60. "TV Violence Is Harmful," Reader's Digest 102, No. 612 (April 1973): 45.

61. New York Times, October 4, 1969.

62. "Kramer Firm Lands $400,000," Broadcasting, May 1, 1972, p. 39.

63. Citizens Communications Center, Statement of Purpose (Washington, D.C.: Citizens Communications Center, 1970).

64. Ibid.

65. Citizens Communications Center, Progress Report (Washington, D.C.: Citizens Communications Center, 1971).

66. Citizens Communications Center, Statement of Purpose, op. cit.

67. Citizens Communications Center, Progress Report, op. cit.

68. "McGraw Hill Sets Record for Concessions to Minorities," Broadcasting, May 15, 1972, p. 25.

69. Ibid.

70. "The Pool of Experts on Access," Broadcasting, September 20, 1971, p. 37.

71. "Kramer Firm Lands $400,000," Broadcasting, May 1, 1972, p. 39.

72. "Distinct Dislike for Financial Disclosure," Broadcasting, September 6, 1971, p. 39.

73. "Has the Public Benefited From 'Public Participation'?," TV Guide, February 17, 1973, p. 20.

74. Broadcasting, July 2, 1973, p. 22.

75. Ibid., p. 24.

76. Broadcasting, September 20, 1971, op. cit.

77. "Signs of Changing Times in Renewals," Broadcasting, May 20, 1971, p. 35.

78. "The Specialists in Intervention," Broadcasting, May 29, 1972, p. 18.

79. Nicholas Johnson, How To Talk Back To Your Television Set (New York: Bantam Books, 1970), p. 131.

6

AN ASSESSMENT:
WHAT DOES IT
ALL MEAN?

The conference at the White House and the broadcasters plus the citizens' group request for a meeting described in Chapter 4 suggested the extent to which government officials, broadcasters, and citizens' bodies have attached significance to license renewal challenges by citizens' groups. That the movement reached that level suggested that citizens' groups could and have influenced both government policy as well as broadcast industry decisions. Participatory democracy applied to the broadcast industry, as this study has attempted to explore, apparently has had an impact.

This final chapter will summarize the preceding areas and present several recommendations for further study to suggest how the findings outlined in this investigation could be applied in establishing a model citizens' council.

DEVELOPMENT OF GROUPS

As discussed in Chapter 1, citizen participation and concern for commercial broadcasting is not a new phenomenon in this country. Its origins can be traced back into the 1920s. Early citizens' groups led to the establishment of a nationwide network of radio listener councils, which were supported by the NAB. The council movement was approved by both broadcasters and the FCC.

Unfortunately, however, many of the councils did not represent all segments of their communities. They were composed of representatives of Parent-Teachers Associations, church groups, and other civic organizations representing middle class society. The result was that groups from the lower stratum of society or of local communities

were not represented. Moreover, some of the radio listening councils
were not engaged actively in helping to promote a more effective use
of radio. Although some groups were effective, others met on a casual
basis or used the councils for social or expressive purposes.

Regardless of the effectiveness of the groups, the NAB in 1948
apparently viewed the establishment of such a citizens' group network
as a potential threat, and in 1948 discontinued the position of NAB
Listener Council Coordinator.

The radio listening council network also lost its momentum
during World War II as the entire nation, including the broadcast
industry, supported the war effort. That momentum never was re-
gained as the rise of television also served to divert attention from
the radio council concept.

In the 1950s, television matured; and the FCC entered a quiescent
period, recovering from the attacks it received from issuing the "Blue
Book" in 1946. But beginning in late 1959 and into the early 1960s,
certain segments of the public became involved with consumer interests
and problems. This was also the period when the quiz show scandals
erupted; and public attention focused on the broadcast (television) industry, as well as "payola" involving radio stations.

In 1964 the United Church of Christ began its five-year involvement with WLBT-TV in Jackson, Mississippi. As noted earlier, the
United States Court of Appeals in 1969 gave a citizens' group legal
standing to challenge FCC decisions.

Since that year with increased interest in consumerism and
the allocation of public resources—the airwaves—the number of
citizens' groups increased considerably. As opposed to the radio
listener panels, which sought to work peacefully with broadcasters,
the citizens' groups of the 1960s and 1970s used whatever means short
of violence to compel a station to comply with their demands.

Usually the demands centered on lack of programming for racial
minorities in communities; lack of awareness, consultation, or ascertainment of the needs and interests of such minorities; and failure
to employ racial minorities. Citizens' coalitions and citizens' groups
appeared to prefer filing petitions to deny the renewal of a station's
license with the FCC than to communicate directly with the station
manager on a person-to-person basis.

TYPES OF COUNCILS

Using the challenge or the threat of a challenge to deny a license
as its principal leverage, citizens' groups then offered to negotiate
with the station asking the licensee to comply with their requests in

exchange for withdrawing the petition to deny. In many instances, the challengers were successful. But in some cases, the stations contested the challenges, resulting in a backlog of pending hearings for the FCC and in time-consuming litigation efforts by the stations.

There were several types of citizens' groups. Historically, the early groups operated on a local basis; and broadcasters occasionally would participate in their meetings, such as with the Portland (Oregon) Listening Council. There were also early national groups with local chapters such as the National Federation of Women. A few groups were formed during the 1945-60 period such as the American Council for Better Broadcasting, the National Association for Better Broadcasting, and the Wisconsin Radio Television Council.

This study examined the Greater Cleveland Radio and Television Council, which was formed in 1940 and still exists. It earned the respect of local broadcasters and has a high membership, although most of the members are women. It was selected as a local, non-militant group that was well organized.

Also examined was Action for Children's Television, a group formed in 1968 with specific goals. ACT operates on a national basis and is an aggressive organization that has not hesitated to petition or confront both local broadcasters and the networks. It also petitioned the FCC. Many of its members are women.

Another citizens' group discussed was the Citizens Communication Center, which has functioned as a legal resource group for other citizens' organizations. CCC is a small firm, composed mainly of attorneys, and has been involved in a number of license renewal challenges across the nation.

There is yet another type of citizens' group not fully examined in this study because of its nature: the transient citizens' coalition group composed of various racial minority group representatives who have joined together to form a legal entity to challenge a station's license. This type of group tends to exist only long enough to accomplish its goals. These groups also have appeared to act militantly toward broadcast licensees. Such organizations have appeared in Portland, Oregon, San Franciso, California, Chicago, Illinois, and in numerous other cities. They probably have accounted for the majority of license renewal challenges. The United Church of Christ, which has been instrumental in assisting such groups, said it has been involved in "hundreds of cases" in which local citizens' groups have requested the church's legal assistance.

This is not to say that all recent citizens' groups are composed of racial minority representatives acting in a militant manner. But it would probably be safe to observe that most of such citizens' coalitions are of that nature.

It could be argued that since the majority of the recent citizens' groups tend to have a transitory nature and to be representative of racial minorities, they therefore would not represent a community or a community's more stable or established constituency. However, because they have represented ethnic groups whose interests apparently have been neglected by broadcasters, such representation also would be their greatest strength. Despite their transitory nature these groups have had an impact, and their influences might well have a long term result.

In many instances, their complaints or the basis of their complaints have been justified—justified to the extent that stations have complied with their requests. As noted in Chapters 3, 4, and 5, such requests or complaints have centered on the following: stations have neglected to ascertain interests and needs of minority publics, stations have failed to air programming reflecting problems of entertainment needs of minority audiences, stations have failed to employ or promote equitably members of racial minorities, stations' transfer of ownership would affect local programming in a negative manner.

BROADCAST INDUSTRY'S RESPONSE

The broadcast industry has reacted in one of several ways as discussed in Chapter 3. Historically, the NAB and individual broadcasters encouraged and supported citizens' groups. Such support, at times, may have been condescending or patronizing. More recently, the broadcast industry and the NAB have viewed citizens' groups in a hostile if not fearful manner. Understandably, the NAB sought actions from Congress to amend or revise the Communications Act to extend the three-year license period to five years. It also sought to deny citizens' group challengers the right to apply for a license until an individual licensee lost its FCC authorization to broadcast.

Network executives also tend to speak of citizens' groups in a disparaging and antagonistic manner. The same could be said of state associations of commercial broadcasters.

Yet individual broadcasters have not always reacted in a similar manner. In several cases cited in Chapter 5, stations, or groups of stations, noted that they have benefited from citizens' groups and their challenges. As one broadcaster stated, "We've been sensitized to the problems of minority groups and their interests." And the president of a multistation organization, Capital Cities, pledged to use $1 million to develop programming for minority groups.

As Chapters 3 and 4 indicated, the amount of locally produced programs has increased within the past two years, possibly as a result of the FCC's prime time ruling on television. But it could be that the increase may have resulted from the broadcasters' awareness and responsiveness to citizens' groups.

One further point needs to be mentioned. It could be argued that this study has depicted the commercial broadcaster as a commercially motivated individual concerned only with profits and not with serving his community and its various publics. Not all broadcasters can be so described. Some station managers and owners are community conscious and make serious efforts to serve and be responsive to their communities. Others, however, are not. And citizens' councils, as noted in Chapter 1, have come into existence in areas where various publics feel the broadcaster may not have provided adequate broadcast service.

Similarly, this study has not intended to indicate that the FCC has been totally or intentionally negligent in its performance. As indicated in Chapter 4, the FCC has adopted regulations designed to benefit the public; and it has issued policies and guidelines such as the "Blue Book" or the "1960 Programming Statement," which broadcasters often have resented.

But just as the commission has acted to help serve the public on occasion, it also has ignored certain facets in broadcasting. The FCC initially refused to recognize legally citizens' groups, and it was only after a court reversed the commission's decision and chastised the agency that the FCC admitted that citizens' groups do represent a public constituency. And the commission's issuing of its procedural manual, "The Public and Broadcasting," suggests a belated awareness and concern for helping citizens' groups.

PARADIGM OF A CITIZENS' GROUP

Theoretically it would be simple to construct a paradigm of an "ideal" or "most efficient" type of citizens' group. Such a model would be composed of representatives of all strata of its community; it would be unbiased, courteous, well-organized, adequately financed, articulate, and so on. But before entering into specific qualifications of such a paradigm, it would be helpful to return to the definitions of citizens' organizations mentioned in Chapter 2.

That chapter pointed out that some of the main functions of a council would include providing citizen input to broadcast stations, providing a vehicle that broadcasters could use as a sounding board, providing a means by which citizens could help stations in programming, explaining to the community the mechanics of broadcasting, providing local public evaluation of programs, and increasing the lines of communication between the broadcasters and their publics. These goals have been achieved by some citizens' groups, but not by all such organizations.

Nevertheless, how should an ideal council be composed? Synthesizing the experiences of the Greater Cleveland Radio and Television Council, Action for Children's Television, and other citizens' groups, such a paradigm would include their best points. The council would be composed of volunteer members of the community and would vary in size, with a membership limit of 100. Members would be from all strata of the community, from women's groups, labor organizations, schools, racial minority groups, religious organizations, civic clubs, business and government groups, and from other institutions such as hospitals.

The initiative for establishing an ideal citizens' group could come from any one of several local institutions, such as local colleges or universities, the chamber of commerce, the local newspaper, members of the local business community, civic organizations, and even from local broadcast stations. The intitial impetus should not originate from a governmental body since broadcasters might fear additional government influence. A citizens' council should be just that, a group of volunteer citizens independent of local, state or federal government.

A paradigm citizens' council would attempt to work with broadcasters on an informal basis. In any type of negotiation it would seem reasonable to keep the lines of communication open at all levels and not to use a third party such as a government agency unless all other means have failed. In some instances, broadcast licensees were not approached by citizens' groups before the groups filed a petition to deny the station's licenses with the FCC. This was apparently why the FCC issued its proposal that citizens' groups and broadcasters should be encouraged to settle their differences privately. In brief, the commission should be consulted only when all other efforts have been exhausted.

Dues and other organizational requirements would be minimal. The group would have stability and meet monthly or perhaps more often. It would also have subcommittees to pursue particular interests. Broadcasters would be invited to attend all meetings but would not have voting privileges such as the Cleveland group permits.

By participating in a citizens' group, members probably would gain a measure of political efficacy at the local level by being involved in the decision-making process to influence programming. Ideally, this would establish for the individual a sense of citizen duty and responsibility and would help offset the feeling of apathy found in many communities.

One of the problems an ideal group should attempt to avoid is having its leadership and goals selected or determined by special interest groups. In Chapter 2, it was noted that sociological studies have indicated that voluntary associations tend to be composed mainly of well-educated persons, and that the less well educated tend not to participate in civic matters. This could pose problems for a model broadcast council. Hopefully, this could be circumvented by having labor organizations and community action groups encourage participation.

Another potential problem area would involve gaining the co-operation and respect of broadcasters. Some station managers have raised the issue that citizens' groups could become potential censors. Such a possibility could occur, especially if the group were dominated by special interest factions or representatives. But the experiences of the early radio listening councils and other groups suggest that the censorship issue was not a problem.

There are other disadvantages and possible problems involved that have been described in earlier chapters. These include general apathy by working members of the group, the possibility of stations using the council as a type of showcase for public relations, resentment or hostility by the broadcasters who might attempt to co-op the group's goals, and the possible domination of the council by certain types of members who are better educated and who might represent only special self interests. Also, the effectiveness of the council's functions could be circumvented, frustrated, or thwarted by broadcasters. This would depend on the council's efficiency, membership, and leadership.

IMPLICATIONS

The question could be asked: "What does all this mean? What are the implications of the emergence or reemergence of citizens' groups?" There are several implications that can be placed into several categories.

The first category involves the various publics and their dissatisfaction with commercial broadcasting. Members of some of these publics have formed citizens' groups to express their dissatisfaction and to take positive action. Through an increased interest and the growth of citizen awareness that the airwaves are a public resource, members of these publics are taking action, exercising their right to express their views on how the airwaves should be used and who should or should not hold a broadcast license. Moreover, the presence and visibility of a citizens' group in one community could enhance the possibilities of similar organizations forming in nearby communities. To use a cliche, "success breeds success." As a result of the WLBT-TV decision, other groups have formed taking advantage of the legal precedents created in that decision. Public dissatisfaction with commercial broadcasting has led to public participation in broadcast matters.

The second implication centers on the broadcast industry and how it has responded to public participation. The broadcast industry has been affected and has taken action. The industry has employed more members of racial minorities, it has begun to question accepted and traditional methods of surveying community leaders, and it has given more thought to how the stations should ascertain the needs of more community groups—including minority publics.

Broadcast stations have revised policies and guidelines. That the NAB codes have reduced the suggested number of commercials for children is one of these revisions. These changes most likely will continue as long as citizens' groups remain active. Should public participation and citizens' organizations lose their momentum, stations may revert to earlier policies, since it obviously would be more profitable for them to reduce local programming and personnel.

Related to these two categories would be the third. Both broadcasters and citizens' groups are learning from each other. Each needs to learn how to ask intelligent questions about the other. Some of the experiences of citizens' groups and their discussions with broadcasters mentioned in this study indicate that station managers are becoming aware of the needs and problems of citizens as expressed through such organizations, and group members are learning the problems and mechanics of operating a station.

A fourth implication involves the FCC. Just as stations have adopted new guidelines, the FCC has formed new regulations and issued new publications. That the commission is concerned with children's television programs and is considering the establishment of a special office to help citizens' groups tends to support the observation that the FCC is changing. It seems likely that the commission will continue to adopt new policies and regulations to assist public participation.

Another category of implication is from a political perspective. Broadcasters are seeking sympathy, if not relief, from citizens' group challenges in a political context. That broadcast industry leaders met with a U.S. president to enlist his support and that Clay Whitehead, former director of the Office of Telecommunications Policy, repeatedly suggested when he was in office that the license renewal period be extended from three to five years indicate that public participation has indeed become a political issue. Whitehead also urged that the 1934 Communications Act be amended to force local stations to be held accountable for program content and balance, including the programs of national networks. If the act were to be amended along those lines, the position of local citizens' groups probably would be enhanced—assuming that the stations would work with groups and assuming that citizens' groups are viable. Some members of Congress apparently chose to assist the broadcasters in a different manner: to extend the license period—which could assist them by providing more time, two years, to improve their services.

The last implication is from a historical viewpoint; the broadcast history appears to be repeating itself. The NAB actively encourated the formation of a nationwide network of radio listening councils in the late 1930s. Now, nearly 40 years later, the NAB is again slowly becoming cognizant of the importance and potential value (or threat) of citizen feedback and citizen participation in broadcasting. The NAB, although gradually and indirectly, probably will not discourage citizen participation. As an industry group, it cannot afford openly and directly to encourage citizens' groups. But it may be forced to realize that it has to learn to live with and cooperate with such organizations. Consumerism is too strong to reject flatly, and commercial broadcasters most likely realize they would be wise to cooperate with such groups if they wish to retain their licenses.

Then there is the question of who speaks for the public. One possible answer was advanced that no one speaks for the public; the public is composed of many diverse and minority publics. The implication here is that citizens' groups have proven that their organizations can speak for one type of public and the organizations they represent.

If enough people become involved with participating groups to the extent of influencing broadcasters, it would seem a reasonable observation that advertisers, advertising agencies, and other segments of society that help support the broadcast industry would have to become aware of the changes prompted by citizens' groups and their potential influence. This could lead to an altering of the traditional relationship between the advertiser and the broadcaster. Related to this future relationship is how the courts will continue to define the fairness doctrine and whether countercommercials and access to the air are granted to citizens' groups and to other organizations interested in promoting their goals.

Other nations such as Japan and Great Britain use citizens' panels to assist broadcast programming. Since the FCC formally has endorsed citizens' groups, it seems that the broadcast media and those concerned with broadcasting should attempt to learn more about them. Individual broadcasters, the NAB, and the FCC should encourage actively continued and increased growth of citizen participation. Instituions of higher learning also could encourage and play a supporting role in the establishment of citizens' groups.

Central to this investigation has been the assumption cited in Chapter 1 that stated that public participation in broadcast matters can provide a valid link between the broadcaster and the various publics and that such participation is a real concern to broadcasters who have tended to organize themselves for protection from citizens' groups. This book and its implications have indicated that the experiences of citizens' groups in this country do provide the link between citizens and broadcasters.

In line with this, several final conclusions are offered. First, because of the value and benefit gained from the link between citizens and broadcasters, both the FCC and broadcasters need to adopt new attitudes and policies to encourage citizen participation. The data offered in this study indicate that most of the recent major changes in broadcasting have occurred only when members of the public have taken legal or formal action. Indeed, the FCC and most broadcasters opposed many of the proposed changes. The commission refused to grant legal standing to citizens' groups, and most broadcasters opposed the reduction of commercials for children and the elimination of cigarette commercials. The FCC and the broadcast industry generally have ignored or belittled citizens' groups initially. But after such groups have obtained greater visibility and financial and legal support, the commission and the broadcasters have adopted a different posture.

It is understandable but unfortunate that most broadcasters and network officials do not have a more receptive attitude toward citizens' groups. Some broadcasters apparently have tolerated and used citizens' groups purely for public relations purposes to impress the FCC at license renewal periods. If broadcasters did adopt new policies and attitudes toward citizens' groups, it would entail a whole-hearted commitment. This means endorsing and encouraging citizen participation both publicly and privately. Some broadcasters cited in this study privately worked with groups but publicly opposed them. It is this type of attitude which needs to be changed.

Second, if the broadcasters continue their present policy of opposing citizen participation, then it would be incumbent on the FCC to enforce rigidly the 1934 Communications Act and the "Blue Book." Both clearly state that broadcasters will serve "the public interest, convenience and necessity." Other FCC regulations and policies could also be more strongly enforced such as the 1960 Programming Statement. As this study has pointed out, the commission since 1960 has been more active in emphasizing that broadcasters have an obligation to serve many publics and to invite public comments. Yet more needs to be done. The American Civil Liberties Union, as mentioned earlier, suggested that the FCC should create local offices to work with citizens' groups to evaluate local stations. This suggestion has merit. Also, the commission should consider using other

forms of mass media such as newspapers, magazines, and films
to encourage citizen participation and comments on the performance
of local broadcast stations.

Finally, the 1934 Communications Act may need to be reevaluated
and revised. To regulate a dynamic and complex industry with a 40-
year-old law, despite amendments, does not speak well for the whole
system. As communications attorney Marcus Cohn suggested, perhaps the act ought to be revised to reward stations that have performed
in an admirable mannter by lengthening their license periods. Similarly, stations that abused the airwaves could have their license
periods shortened. Also, perhaps the act should be revised to require
stations to work with citizens' groups and invite public participation.

Given the importance of broadcasting and given the value of
public participation in that area, it would seem reasonable to conclude
that if the momentum of the consumer movement continues at the rate
with which it has been sustained in the last decade, citizens' councils
could have a pivotal role in the future of broadcasting.

SELECTED BIBLIOGRAPHY

BOOKS

Almond, Gabriel, and Sidney Verba. The Civic Culture. Princeton: Princeton University Press, 1962.

Ackerman, William. Time For Reason About Radio. New York: George S. Steward, Publishers, 1948.

Barnouw, Erik. The Golden Web. New York: Oxford University Press, 1968.

Bauer, Raymond, Itheil De Sola Pool and L. A. Dexter. American Business and Public Policies. New York: Atherton Press, 1963.

Brown, Les. Television, The Business Behind the Box. New York: Harcourt, Brace, Jovanovich, 1971.

Gillmor, Donald, and Jerrome Barron. Supplement to Mass Communications Law. St. Paul: West Publishing Co., 1971.

Head, Sydney. Broadcasting in America, A Survey of Television-Radio. Boston: Houghton Mifflin Co., 1972.

Hill, Frank Ernest, and W. E. Williams. Radio's Listening Groups: The United States and Great Britain. New York: Columbia University Press, 1941.

Johnson, Nicholas. How To Talk Back To Your Television Set. New York: Bantam Books, 1970.

Kahn, Frank. Documents of American Broadcasting. New York: Appleton-Century-Crofts, 1968.

Larsen, Otto. Violence and The Mass Media. New York: Harper & Row, 1968.

Lazarsfeld, Paul, and Harry Field. The People Look at Radio. Chapel Hill: University of North Carolina Press, 1946.

_____ and Patricia Kendall, Radio Listening in America, The People Look at Radio Again. New York: Prentice-Hall, 1948.

Lipset, Seymour. Political Man. New York: Doubleday, 1960.

MacAvoy, Paul. The Crisis of the Regulatory Commissions. New York: W. W. Norton and Co., 1970.

Pearson, Drew. The Case Against Congress. New York: Pocket Books, 1969.

Pfiffner, John, and Robert Presthus. Public Administration. New York: The Ronald Press Co., 1967.

Randall, Richard. Censorship of The Movies. Madison: University of Wisconsin, 1967.

Rivers, William, Willima Blankenburg, William Starck, and Earl Reeves. Back Talk: Press Councils in America. San Francisco: Canfield Press, 1972.

Olson, Joe. Education On The Air. 20th Yearbook of The Institute for Education by Radio. Columbus: The Ohio State University Press, 1950.

_____. Education On The Air. 23rd Yearbook of The Institute for Education by Radio. Columbus: The Ohio State University Press, 1953.

Rivers, William, Theodore Peterson, and Jay Jensen. The Mass Media and Modern Society. San Francisco: Rinehart Press, 1971.

Roberts, Edwin. The Smut Rakers. Silver Spring: The National Observer, 1966.

Siepmann, Charles. Radio, Television and Society. New York: Oxford University Press, 1960.

Seldes, Gilbert. The New Mass Media. Washington, D. C.: Public Affairs Press, 1968.

Skornia, Harry. Television and Society. New York: McGraw-Hill Co., 1965.

_____. Sound and Television Broadcasting in Britain. London:
     Her Majesty's Stationery Office, 1969.

Summers, Robert, and Harrison Summers. Broadcasting and The
     Public. Belmont, California: Wadsworth Publishing Co., 1967.

Stavins, Ralph. Television Today: The End of Communication and
     The Death of Community. Washington, D.C.: Institute for
     Policy Studies, 1969.

Steiner, Gary. The People Look at Television: A Study of Audience
     Attitudes. New York: Alfred A. Knopf, 1963.

Taishoff, Sol, ed. Broadcasting Yearbook 1973. Washington, D.C.:
     Broadcasting Publications, Inc., 1973.

Verba, Sidney. Small Groups and Political Behavior. Princeton:
     Princeton University Press, 1961.

Waller, Judith. Radio, The Fifth Estate, New York: Houghton-Mifflin
     Co., 1948.

Weinberg, Meyer. TV in America. New York: Ballantine Books,
     1962.

White, Llewellyn. The American Radio, A Report on The Broadcast
     Industry in The United States from The Commission on Freedom
     of the Press. Chicago: University of Chicago Press, 1947.

Williams, Albert. Listening, A Collection of Critical Attitudes.
     Denver: University of Denver Press, 1948.

                        MAGAZINES AND JOURNALS

Baldwin, Thomas, F., and Stuart Surlin. "A Study of Broadcast
     Station License Application Exhibits on Ascertainment of Com-
     munity Needs." Journal of Broadcasting 14 (spring, 1970): 164.

Broadcasting
          "Johnson Praises FCC Concern for Consumer," February 1,
              1971, p. 44.
          "Signs of Changing Times in Renewals," May 17, 1971, p. 34.
          "Distinct Dislike For Financial Disclosure," September 6, 1971,
              p. 39.

"Hard Times: FCC's Yearly Accounting," June 19, 1971, p. 31.

"At FCC: More Aid to Challengers," July 5, 1971, p. 47.

"Broadcasters' Pre-Emptive Court," August 30, 1971, p. 17.

"Paradoxical Time in Children's TV," September 13, 1971, p. 15.

"The Struggle Over Broadcast Access," September 20, 1971, pp. 32-43.

"The Pool of Experts on Access," September 20, 1971, p. 36.

"The Struggle Over Broadcast Access (II), September 27, 1971, p. 24.

"Settling In: Mrs. Roberts and Dr. Pearce," October 4, 1971, pp. 36-37.

"Relief is Just a Senate Bill Away," October 11, 1971, p. 49.

"NAB Looks to FCC for Renewal Relief," October 25, 1971, p. 24.

"Hope From The Hill on Renewal Relief," November 8, 1971, p. 41.

"Undaunted ACT Bends The FTC's Ear," November 15, 1971, p. 26.

"Ascertaining Needs of Broadcasters," November 29, 1971, p. 63.

"Two After Deadline File Petitions," December 6, 1971, p. 30.

"ACT Goes Back to The FTC," December 20, 1971, pp. 45-6.

"Burch: Welcome Mat Always Out At FCC," January 10, 1972, p. 47.

"Wholesale Attack in San Francisco," January 31, 1972, p. 29.

"Minorities Get Office at NAB," May 1, 1972, p. 41.

"Challenges From All Sides in New York Renewals," May 8, 1972, p. 32.

"McGraw-Hill Sets Record for Concessions to Minorities," May 15, 1972, p. 36.

"Any Ceiling Now in Sight on the Settling of Sale Protests?" May 29, 1972, p. 18.

"The Specialists in Intervention," May 29, 1972, p. 18.

"WWJ-TV, WTCJ Renewed," June 5, 1972, p. 10.

"Citizen Shakedown Asserted in Rochester," June 19, 1972, p. 41.

"Bartley Looks Back 20 Years from FCC Doorway," June 26, 1972, p. 34.

"Court Backs FCC on WMAL Renewal," July 3, 1972, p. 6.

"A Swing Back: Court Stiffens on Protests to Renewals," July 10, 1972, p. 17.

"Hear, Hear," July 10, 1972, p. 60.

"Wiley Likes WMAL Decision," July 17, 1972, p. 32.

"30 Stations Queried on Employment Records," July 31, 1972, p. 37.

"Compensation to Challengers: Blackmail or Part of the Process," September 18, 1972, p. 24.

"NAB is Thumbs-Down on Payments to Challenger," October 2, 1972, pp. 35-6.

"When Do Challenges Become 'Extortion?' " October 9, 1972, p. 31.

"Hooks Starts Delivering on His Commitment to Blacks," October 9, 1972, p. 31.

"The Dust Hasn't Settled After Speech by Whitehead," January 1, 1973, p. 18.

"Cleaning Up Radio," Business Week, May 18, 1935, p. 25.

"Radio Critics." Business Week, August 10, 1935, p. 23.

Cohn, Marcus. "Should The FCC Reward Stations That Do A Good Job." Saturday Review, August 14, 1971, p. 45.

"Where, May We Ask, Was the FCC?" Consumer Reports, January 1960, pp. 9-11.

"Here, We Would Suggest, Is A Program For The FCC." Consumer Reports, February 1960, p. 93.

"Making FCC's Mission Impossible." Consumer Reports, February 1970, p. 110.

Crosby, John. "Radio and Who Makes It." The Atlantic Monthly, January 1948, p. 24.

"Markle Grants for Studies Seek Quality in Journalism," Editor & Publisher, April 22, 1972, p. 46.

Ehrich, Thomas. "Our Troubled Stations." Columbia Journalism Review 11 (July-August 1972): 43.

Emery, Walter. "Broadcasting Rights and Responsibilities in A Democratic Society." The Centennial Review of Arts and Science, 1964, p. 320.

"The Revolt Against Radio." Fortune, March 1948, p. 175.

Gans, Herbert. "The New Egalitarianism." Saturday Review, May 6, 1972, p. 46.

Goldstein, Walter. "Network Television and Political Change: Two Issues in Democratic Theory." Western Political Quarterly 20 (December 1967): 884-5.

Guimary, Donald. "Oregon Television, Radio Stations Weigh Public Tastes." The Oregon Broadcaster 17 (January 1972): 2.

"The Texarkana Agreement as a Model Strategy for Citizen Participation on FCC License Renewals." Harvard Journal on Legislation 7 (May 1970): 885.

Jacoby, Arthur, and Nicholas Babchuck. "Instrumental and Expressive Voluntary Association." Sociology and Social Research 27 (July 1963): 213.

Krause, Elliot. "Functions of a Bureaucratic Ideology: Citizen Participation." Social Problems 16 (fall 1968): 129.

Lewis, Dorothy. "The Listener's Stake in American Radio." Broadcasting, July 13, 1942, p. 66.

"The Heaviest Viewers Are The 'Lonely and Alienated.' " Life, September 10, 1971, pp. 42-3.

"Cluster of Awards for Programs." Literary Digest, May 2, 1936, p. 34.

Mayer, Martin. "Has the Public Benefited by 'Public Participation?' " TV Guide, February 18, 1973, pp. 18-21.

"Death of an Industry?" Nation's Business, May 1972, p. 28.

"The American Corporation Under Fire." Newsweek, May 18, 1971, pp. 74-85.

"Blacks vs. Broadcasters." Newsweek, June 19, 1972, p. 84.

"Your Kids Need Better TV—You Can Help." Parade, January 20, 1972, pp. 20-1.

Shayon, Robert Lewis. "Act with ACT." Saturday Review, March 7, 1970, p. 22.

_____. "Collision Course." Saturday Review, August 7, 1971, p. 38.

_____. "Caveat Pre-Empter." Saturday Review, January 9, 1971, p. 37.

_____. "Fairness Deferred." Saturday Review, April 29, 1972, p. 23.

Seldes, Gilbert. "Public Participation." The Public Opinion Quarterly 24 (fall 1963): 9.

"Boston Tea Party—1970." TV Guide, July 4, 1970.

Sigal, Roberta. "Citizens Committees—Advice vs. Consent." Transaction, May 1967, p. 48.

Television/Radio Age
    "Inside The FCC," February 22, 1971, p. 78.
    "Inside The FCC," March 8, 1971, pp. 61-2.
    "Inside The FCC," March 22, 1971, p. 98.
    "Inside The FCC," June 14, 1971, p. 60.
    "Inside The FCC," April 3, 1972, pp. 62-3.
    "Access Rule Increases Station Originations," July 24, 1972, pp. 21-4.
    "Inside The FCC," August 21, 1972, pp. 75-6.
    "Inside The FCC," October 30, 1972, p. 78.

Wright, Charles. "Voluntary Association Memberships of American Adults: Evidence From National Sample Surveys." American Sociological Review 23 (June 1958): 286.

NEWSPAPERS

New York Times, October 4, 1969.

Eugene Register-Guard, July 5, 1971.

Eugene Register-Guard, October 6, 1971.

The Oregonian, October 13, 1971.

The Oregonian, January 4, 1972.

The Cleveland Press, May 4, 1972.

Oregon Journal, May 25, 1972.

Oregon Journal, June 7, 1972.

The Oregonian, July 9, 1972.

Oregon Journal, July 28, 1972.

The Oregonian, July 24, 1972.

Wall Street Journal, October 22, 1970.

GOVERNMENT DOCUMENTS

U.S., Federal Communications Commission. Report and Statement of Policy, Network Programming Inquiry. Washington, D.C., 1960.

U.S., Federal Communications Commission. Letter to Station KTAL-TV, FCC 690827, and accompanying statement by Commissioner Nicholas Johnson, July 29, 1969.

U.S., Federal Communications Commission. Notice of Inquiry and Notice of Proposed Rule Making. Docket 18859, Washington, D.C., May 18, 1970.

U.S., Federal Communications Commission. The FCC in Fiscal 1969. Washington, D.C.: Government Printing Office, 1970.

U.S., Federal Communications Commission. Primer on Ascertainment of Community Problems by Broadcast Applicants. Federal Register, March 3, 1971.

U.S., Federal Communications Commission. FCC Reports. Docket 18774, Washington, D.C., February 18, 1971.

U.S., Federal Communications Commission. The FCC in Fiscal 1971. Washington, D.C.: Government Printing Office, 1972.

U.S., Federal Communications Commission. The Public and Broadcasting, Procedural Manual. Federal Register, Part III, September 29, 1972.

INTERVIEWS

William Mears, public affairs director, KOIN-AM-FM-TV, Portland, Oregon, October 18, 1972.

William Ray, chief, Complaints and Compliances Division, Federal Communications Commission, November 5, 1971.

CORRESPONDENCE

Baze, Ted, program director, WUAB-TV, Cleveland, Ohio, June 22, 1972.

Bishop, Lee, executive secretary, Oregon Association of Broadcasters, July 25, 1972.

Danish, Roy, director, Television Information Office, January 6, 1970.

Dougherty, Joseph, president, Broadcast Division, Capital Cities Broadcasting, September 29, 1972.

Goldberg, Henry, assistant counsel, Office of Telecommunications Policy, August 24, 1972.

Helffrich, Stockton, director, Code Authority, National Association of Broadcasters, July 6, 1972.

Hooks, Benjamin, commissioner, Federal Communications Commission, September 27, 1972.

Hoover, J. T., manager, Audience Information, American Broadcasting Company, December 28, 1970.

Kasmire, Robert, vice president for corporation information, National Broadcasting Company, December 10, 1970.

Lewis, Dorothy, Listening Council coordinator, National Association of Broadcasters, January 27, 1971.

Matkovick, A. J., former president, Greater Cleveland Radio and Television Council, June 29, 1971.

Palmer, Dorothy, former president, Minnesota Radio Council,
    February 17, 1970.

Perris, Donald L., general manager, WEWS-TV, Cleveland, Ohio,
    June 27, 1972.

Sarson, Evelyn, president, Action for Children's Television, June 7,
    1972.

Slough, E., historian, Greater Cleveland Radio and Television
    Council, June 13, 1972.

Spinrad, Leonard, director of corporate information, Columbia Broad-
    casting System, December 16, 1970.

Varholy, Joe, program manager, WKYC-TV, Cleveland, Ohio,
    June 28, 1972.

Wiley, Richard E., commissioner, Federal Communications Com-
    mission, October 12, 1972.

OTHER SOURCES

Action for Children's Television. ACT Newsletter 1, January-February
    1970.

_____. ACT Newsletter 3, summer 1970.

_____. ACT Newsletter 4, summer 1972.

Burch, Dean. "Comments." Speech to American Advertising Federa-
    tion, Washington, D.C., February 2, 1971.

Capital Cities Broadcasting Corporation. Policy Statement filed with
    Federal Communications Commission, fall 1972.

Center for the Study of Democratic Institutions. Bureaucracy and
    the Forests. (Santa Barbara: Center for the Study of Democratic
    Institutions, 1962).

_____. Broadcasting and Government Regulation in a Free Society.
    (Santa Barbara: Center for the Study of Democratic Institutions,
    1959).

Citizens Communications Center. Statement of Purpose. Washington,
    D.C., September 1970.

Danish, Roy. "Broadcast Freedom—Is It Still There?" Speech to
    Poor Richard's Club, Philadelphia, Pennsylvania, November
    11, 1971.

Gale, Richard. "From Sit-In to Hike-In: A Comparison of Civil Rights
    and Environmental Movements." Unpublished manuscript at
    Harper & Row, New York, 1972.

Greater Cleveland Radio and Television Council. Regulations.
    Cleveland: Greater Cleveland Radio and Television Council,
    April 1971.

_____. Standing Rules Cleveland: Greater Cleveland Radio and
    Television Council, March 1971.

Jencks, Richard. "Broadcast Regulation by Private Contract: Some
    Observations on 'Community Control' of Broadcasting." Speech
    to Broadcasting Industry Symposium. Washington, D.C.,
    January 18, 1971.

Johnson, Nicholas, "Government by Television: A Case Study Per-
    spectives and Proposals." Speech to International Association of
    Political Consultants, London, England, December 14, 1970.

Lewis, Dorothy. Radio and Public Service. A Guidebook for Radio
    Chairmen. New York: National Association of Broadcasters,
    1944.

Lowenstein, Ralph. "Has AEJ Proved The Case for a National Press
    Council?" Paper presented to the Association for Education in
    Journalism, Berkeley, California, August 25, 1969.

Mt. Hood Broadcasting Corporation. KOIN Policy Statement, filed
    with the Federal Communications Commission, February, 1972.

National Association of Broadcasters. Code News. New York:
    National Association of Broadcasters, January 1972.

_____. Code News. New York: National Association of Broadcasters,
    May 1972.

_____. Study Guide on Broadcasting. New York: National Association
    of Broadcasters, 1966.

_____. The Television Code, New York: National Association of Broadcasters, 1972.

Portland Radio Council. Annual Report. Portland, Oregon, 1943.

Rule, Elton. Speech to California Broadcasters Association, Palm Springs, California, January 27, 1972.

Smith, Ralph. "A Study of The Professional Criticism of Broadcasting In The United States, 1920-1955." Unpublished doctoral dissertation, University of Wisconsin, 1959.

Spence, Leslie. Radio Listening. Madison, Wisconsin: Wisconsin Joint Committee for Better Radio Listening, 1946.

Whitehead, Clay. "Remarks." Speech to Ohio Association of Broadcasters, Columbus, Ohio, September 29, 1971.

_____. "Remarks." Speech to International Radio and Television Society, New York, October 6, 1971.

_____. "Remarks." Speech to Sigma Delta Chi Luncheon, Indianapolis, Indiana, December 18, 1972.

DONALD L. GUIMARY is Associate Professor of Journalism at Portland State University in Oregon. During 1973-74, he was a lecturer in mass communications at Universiti Sains Malaysia at Penang, Malaysia. While in that part of the world he observed other broadcast and media systems and participated in UNESCO and United States Information Service broadcast seminars in Kuala Lumpur and Saigon.

Dr. Guimary has published in the area of broadcast and print communications. His articles have appeared in Journalism Quarterly, Educational Broadcasting Review, The Quill, The Oregonian, and other publications.

Dr. Guimary holds a Ph.D. from the University of Oregon.

RELATED TITLES
Published by
Praeger Special Studies

THE ELECTRONIC BOX OFFICE: Humanities and
Arts on the Cable
>> Richard Adler
>> Walter S. Baer

FOREIGN AFFAIRS NEWS AND THE BROADCAST
JOURNALIST
>> Robert M. Batscha

GETTING TO SESAME STREET: Origins of the
Children's Television Workshop
>> Richard M. Polsky

PUBLIC ACCESS CABLE TELEVISION IN THE
UNITED STATES AND CANADA: With an Annotated
Bibliography
>> Gilbert Gillespie

THE USES OF COMMUNICATION IN DECISION-
MAKING: A Comparative Study of Yugoslavia
and the United States
>> Alex S. Edelstein